11/9?

BULFINCH ARCHITECTURE/TRAVEL SERIES

# AN ARCHITECT'S

D1304837

WITHDRAWN

# AN ARC

BULFINCH ARCHITECTURE/TRAVEL SERIES

# HITECT'S

# Paris

Thomas Carlson-Reddig

Illustrations by
Thomas and Kelly Carlson-Reddig

A BULFINCH PRESS BOOK
Little, Brown and Company
Boston   Toronto   London

## Acknowledgments

I would like to thank the following people: Brian Hotch-
kiss, from Bulfinch Press, for his keen editing, but more
important for his encouragement and faith in such a book;
Jung/Brannen Associates, Inc., for their support and understanding; my families, for their inquiries, enthusiasm, and
love; and my wife, not only for her resplendent love and
support, but also for her major contributions to this book.

First Edition

## Library of Congress Cataloging-in-Publication Data

Carlson-Reddig, Thomas.
      An architect's Paris / Thomas Carlson-Reddig. — 1st ed.
        p.   cm. — (Bulfinch architecture/travel series)
      Includes bibliographical references.
      ISBN 0-8212-1953-7
       1. Architecture—France—Paris—Themes, motives.
    2. Paris (France)—Buildings, structures, etc.—Guidebooks.
    3. Paris (France)—Description and travel—Guidebooks.
    I. Title. II. Series.
    NA1050.C32   1993
    720′.94436—dc20              92-36977

Bulfinch Press is an imprint and trademark of
Little, Brown and Company (Inc.)
Published simultaneously in Canada by
Little, Brown & Company (Canada) Limited

PRINTED IN HONG KONG

*To my wife, Kelly*

# Contents

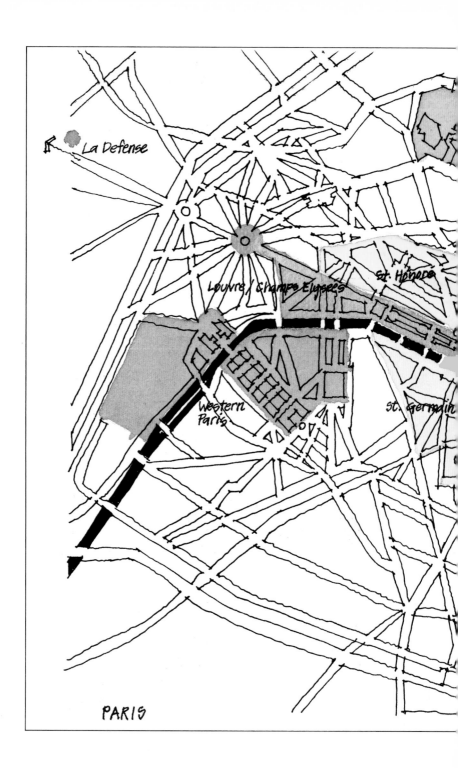

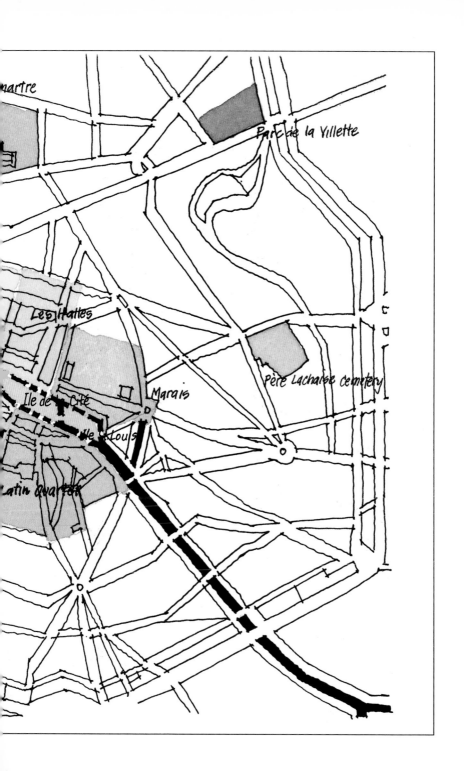

# Introduction

*I*n Paris, romance supersedes the daily
activities of life, dreams overcome reality, and memories are created with
every step. One rarely walks directly but more often circuitously. In the
beginning there may be a destination, but in the end it has changed. Un-
expected discoveries unfold, but the towers of history redirect, so one does
not become lost, except perhaps in a solitary dreaminess. Streets climb and
descend, wind and sever, narrow and broaden, yet a cohesive clarity unifies
the neighborhoods. To the northwest, northeast, and south cranes and
modern towers rise, each one indistinguishable from the next, destroying
the unity of what appears from a distance to be the characterless mass of
an old and deteriorating city. Yet in the near and distant future the center
of Paris will remain, while these temporary towers of glass and steel are
replaced by yet taller structures of materials hitherto unknown. Though
they are impressive for a short time, none can outlast the ageless materials
of the earth that compose the buildings in the center of Paris. The material
and the architecture are inseparable—the same. Some buildings age to
reveal wisdom through their bold construction and massive weathered

Hotel de Ville

stone walls, while the thin facades of newer construction peel away revealing nothing but bones. One can only hope our future will behold an architecture that will age with the grace evident in the work of our predecessors.

Paris is a great city that strives to reach everyone. Power and wealth are clearly displayed on the Avenue des Champs Elysées, while modesty and seediness are evident throughout the area of Montmartre. The medieval world of the Marais bleeds into the fast-paced atmosphere surrounding the Pompidou Center. Bohemian life still pervades the ancient Latin Quarter, which abuts the St. Germain area to the west, where art galleries and exquisite shops saturate the narrow streets. Though the Ile de la Cité has been transformed many times throughout Paris's history, the medieval cathedral of Notre Dame has been defiant against all that has come its way, and it remains the spiritual center of the city. Grand squares and boulevards, helping to give foci to the conundrum of streets woven in intricate patterns, allow the city to breathe, while intimate squares, such as the Place des Vosges, offer humans a chance for breath. The Louvre and the Musée d'Orsay overwhelm all those who love art by their sheer abundance and satisfy the hunger of those who yearn to see masterpieces. In contrast, the Marmottan and Rodin museums offer brilliant art away from the hordes at the major museums, permitting the viewer to reflect on and absorb the works in relative peace. There are cafés of all kinds—those that locals regularly frequent in the mornings and late afternoons to socialize with friends, and others that the chic grace with their presence in hopes of being seen. Visiting cafés becomes an integral routine within the daily lives of those who live in or visit Paris. Some are landmarks which history has made more sacred to many than the monuments and cathedrals. Everyone has a favorite café, and often a favorite park or square. These outdoor settings are essential to Paris's livability, offering peace and tranquillity from the noise and busy streets of the city. Finally, there are countless stores throughout the city, many of which are found near the Opéra by Charles Garnier—an area that continues to thrive as the commercial center of Paris as it has for nearly two centuries.

I entered Paris overwhelmed and intimidated by the city's grand-ness and cultural and historical richness, but in only a short while I was swept off my feet with romance. After I returned home, the remembrances became even more dreamy, fantastic when I wrote the following pages. But regardless of such sentimental hyperbole, Paris is a city of openness, where one will find a dynamism and progressiveness harmoniously balanced with tradition, like no other city in the world.

# Ile de la Cité and Ile St. Louis

*T*he Ile de la Cité and the Ile St. Louis are situated in the River Seine, not only near the geographical center of Paris but in the heart of the city as well. It would be rare to traverse the streets across the river on either side without being aware of the islands, which are repeatedly framed by vistas down the narrow medieval streets. Ile de la Cité was settled by Gaul fishermen in 250–200 B.C., but the township was conquered by the Romans in 52 B.C. Though Roman ruins are no longer evident, the island still exudes an ageless character.

At the western edge of Ile de la Cité is Square du Vert Galant, reached via the steps at the base of King Henri IV's statue. The park is very small, but one immediately feels the powerful significance of being near the center of Paris. During my visit it was comfortably settled with tourists and Parisians alike; like all public parks it is also occupied by a few homeless vagabonds, who go almost unnoticed amid such beauty. As is always the case when a city is viewed across water, it is hard to imagine all of its activity. Looking to northwest Paris from the Ile de la Cité, one sees the apparently interminable Louvre Museum, which extends almost as far as the

Pont Neuf

eye can see, with a few interruptions of the roofline marking the additions that have taken place over the years. Farther east on the Right Bank is the puissantly flamboyant Hôtel de Ville (Town Hall). The complexity of its roofline gives the impression of a miniature village. Toward the west, down the lively river that carries tourists and frigates alike, the iron Pont des Arts delicately rests upon its massive stone piers, which are set deep within the Seine. People seem to flow across this popular pedestrian bridge with the same constant motion as the river. On the Left Bank, opposite the Louvre and across the Pont des Arts, is the Institut de France, whose dome interrupts the repetitive rows of six-to-eight-story *hôtels* (apartment buildings) lining the *quais*. And finally there is Place St. Michel, where a noticeable void in the continuous facades is softly filled with large trees. It is a gathering spot for students and bohemian nomads.

Just east of Henri IV's statue, across Place du Pont Neuf, is the secluded, intimately scaled Place Dauphine. It was built in 1607 shortly after the completion of Pont Neuf in honor of the future Louis XIII. In urban concept it was to be designed similarly to Place des Vosges in the Marais area, also erected under the reign of Henri IV. Very few of the original buildings remain, but still there is a magical peacefulness in this square

*Pont Neuf*

like no other in Paris. The triangular courtyard is very simple in nature, with rows of trees spaced equally an automobile's length apart reinforcing the geometry. Only wooden benches interrupt the alignment of the trees. To the east are flower beds and low green shrubs that add color to the hardened brown earthen surface. During one of my last days in Paris, on a dark, late afternoon in early autumn, the square was nearly empty but for two lovers on a bench, facing, but oblivious to, the Palais de Justice (Law Courts). They were silent except for an occasional giggle, barely audible above the subtle, muffled hum of the automobiles crossing Pont Neuf to the west. Occasionally horns beeped, but they were faint in comparison with the sounds of rustling leaves from the swirling winds that blew from the east through what is now the broadest opening of the square. The eastern buildings were torn down in the nineteenth century so that the western facade of the Palais de Justice would be more visible. From the trees, typically shaded from the sun, leaves were falling slowly to the ground or landing on the flowers, which fluttered with the breezes, absorbing glimpses of the sun's warmth before their final days of winter. From the hardened earth, the swirls picked up specks of dust that disintegrated and merged with the air. Few cars passed through, though many were parked around the perimeter; those that did enter drove slowly and quietly before parking or continuing on. A few pedestrians entered as well—some stopped for peaceful solitude; others simply passed through—but never did they walk briskly through Place Dauphine. Like Place des Vosges, Place Dauphine causes one to slow down and absorb the setting. It induces introspection.

A moist coolness from the Seine and the large trees that shade the square make Place Dauphine a comfortable place for peaceful contemplation during the warmer months. But even in the winter, when all the trees have shed their leaves, the sun pours into the small square and provides warmth, while surrounding low buildings buffer the arctic air blowing from the north. Whatever the season, Place Dauphine offers harmony to those who desire it. It is a tranquil haven amid urban hustle, which is a necessary component of any city.

While the *quais* (banks) on the north and south of the island are full of both lovers and loners, the north side of the island is more historically and architecturally interesting. The towers d'Argent and Bonbec are but a couple of punctuations along the massive stone walls enclosing the Palais de Justice. The Tour d'Argent once housed the royal treasures and the Tour Bonbec served as a torture chamber during the Reign of Terror following the Revolution. It is a bit odd that both towers are quite the same in appearance, and yet their functions were completely different.

On the west side of Boulevard du Palais is the main entrance to the Palais de Justice, which also leads to a rather small courtyard where the Gothic jewel Ste. Chapelle awkwardly sits. In the thirteenth century, this church was situated prominently in a much larger court connected to the Palais de St. Louis, but today it is enveloped by the Palais de Justice, which professes above all else Liberté (Freedom), Egalité (Equality), and Fraternité (Brotherhood). Originally much of the complex, designed by Louis Duc in 1858 and inspired by ancient Greek and Roman architecture, must have evoked the spirit of democracy, but today its meaning has changed. In medieval times it was one of the most frequented places in the city, and much of the complex was very public, not unlike government buildings in Washington, D.C. The Palais de Justice today hardly expresses the stated traits, but rather evokes qualities of power, wealth, and disjunction. Nevertheless, it is an impressive work of architecture, whose elegant balance can be seen from Rue de Lutèce to the east. In all its Classical repose and calm it complements and anchors the light flamboyancy of Ste. Chapelle, which towers just beyond its stone walls. Ste. Chapelle's animated spires and gargoyles are so convincing that one would think some of the animals are alive, watching all those who traverse the square below.

In the summer months Ste. Chapelle hosts numerous concerts, advertised at the entrance. Having previously experienced the hordes of tourists snapping pictures, my wife and I decided that an evening of medieval music performed in candlelight would be the perfect way to see Ste. Chapelle. We imagined that music could only elevate the glorious light- and color-filled space, recalling the spirits within and giving life to the religious and historical stories recounted in the stained-glass windows and in each stone that composes the walls.

As we expected, the musical performance was spiritual, haunting,

Cathedral Notre Dame

uplifting, and jovial—all things that good music should be. The program proceeded from Gregorian chants dating from the time of Louis IX's crusades and the construction of Ste. Chapelle in the thirteenth century, to English music of the Elizabethan period, and finally culminated with French music of the sixteenth and seventeenth centuries. Rather than watching the candlelit performers, I gazed at the stained-glass windows, which seemed to breathe life with each chord struck or every word sung. The power of the music combined with the heavenly embodiment of the interior made me forget that I was at a twentieth-century performance. Only when the clapping followed each song was I brought back to reality.

Ste. Chapelle was constructed in an amazingly short period of time during the mid-thirteenth century, and until the Revolution it was purported to contain Christ's crown of thorns in its reliquary. Fortunately, much of its original stone and glass remain. Not unlike many Gothic cathedrals, the stone relief and stained-glass windows reveal stories of the world from the creation of Adam and Eve to the Apocalypse, but what distinguishes Ste. Chapelle from other great Gothic cathedrals is its utter simplicity and lightness. The glass walls are so vibrant with color and brightness that the stone almost disappears. Further accentuating this purity is the absence of interior side aisles and massive columns. Even in comparison with today's advanced architecture of steel and glass, Ste. Chapelle achieves an extraordinary lightness that almost transcends structural logic. One can imagine the power and heavenly symbolism it must have presented when first completed.

To the east of Ste. Chapelle and the Palais de Justice is Rue de Lutèce. Adjacent to this square is one of many splendid Métro entrances—cast-iron-and-glass Art Nouveau masterpieces, designed at the turn of the twentieth century by Hector Guimard. Though few of the glass-covered canopies remain intact, they are still powerful reminders of the importance of the innovative and functional urban design that has marked Paris's history. The Art Nouveau architecture of Guimard and others was rather short-lived, but it represents a period in history in which historical revivalism was challenged, and a new architecture, based on nature, was sought. While much Art Nouveau architecture is criticized for being simply decorative with no substance, the Métro stations are an exception. They were one of the first examples of modular prefabricated design, where the parts were interchangeable and could be used to fit the requirements of any Métro station entrance; however, they were designed with such sophistication that the element of craft is still evident and not overpowered by its modular nature.

The Métro entrance Cité fronts Place Louis Lépine, which is a typical flower-and-plant market, also housed in simple iron-and-glass greenhouses. But on Sundays, this area sports endless cages with a beautiful array of small birds, as well as a variety of seeds and berries, that are sold by locals. During our visit it seemed that each bird displayed color hitherto unknown. While incidental, this experience provided a prelude to our first visit this trip to the cathedral of Notre Dame.

Cathédrale Notre Dame typically is swarming with people, inside and out, making the best time to see the interior during a Sunday morning Mass, when one can at least see the church in relative peace. On our first Sunday morning visit we arrived after Mass had begun, so we remained outside to view the exterior. It was a late, mid-August morning and the sun shone intensely on the south facade, which faces the Square Jean XXIII. I was reminded of our last visit to Notre Dame, when we sat in the park marveling at the exterior's richness and virtuosity, photographing the ornament that animates the surfaces. Again the play of light and shadow made wonderful opportunities for photographs, but there was no need to be redundant. While most people typically gaze with wonder at the front facades and interiors of these wonderful Gothic cathedrals, the sides and rear are often equally or more fascinating. They are much less predictable, more tectonic, and are generally a more honest expression of the structural forces of the soaring buildings. While it is natural to respond to buildings on an emotional and instinctive level, architects frequently go much further to analyze why they like something. The analysis of the expressed logic of construction and structure is one such way of judging buildings.

On another Sunday afternoon, we again visited Notre Dame. We climbed the endless stairs of the northern tower to observe the city from the top of the cathedral. It was a dark day, and black clouds rolled in from

Notre Dame

the south. The changing sky and distant mist enveloped the city and limited the view to its center, with only soft silhouettes of the surrounding modern towers visible through the low clouds. The heavens seemed to be growling at the city while light drops of rain blew down until lightning struck nearby and a waterfall gushed from the sky. We watched the scene below as the Place du Parvis Notre Dame, full of street performers, portraitists, a donkey, and numerous admirers, emptied, all running for shelter under the three portals of the west facade, where they were protected beneath the gaze of apostles.

At the top of Notre Dame one is high above the city, but not so high that the city appears as a plan. The noises from below are still audible, and the details of the buildings are still visible, reminding one that the city is real and not an architectural model. Beyond the surrounding streets and square is an array of roofs, punctuated intermittently by significant monuments that help define the many areas of Paris. Far to the west stands the Eiffel Tower, which was softly silhouetted against the darkening sky behind the still-shimmering, golden dome of the Invalides. Though closer, the Eglise de St. Germain des Prés appeared miniature in comparison with the Eiffel Tower. Its decaying pointed towers conveyed its age and revealed its need to be nurtured. Farther south, the massive asymmetrical towers of St. Sulpice awkwardly bulged from the surrounding slate roofs. Nearly directly east of St. Sulpice, the circular temple called the Panthéon appeared even more grand from the sky than from the streets. Its massive form, free from fancy, demanded one's focus; if one was not aware of its function, it could easily be mistaken for the capitol of Paris.

On the Right Bank the mist also softened the grandness of the Arc de Triomphe, rising beyond the magnificent curved-glass roofs of the Grand Palais and the Petit Palais and surrounded by apartments that appeared like crumbling dots of ruins. The mundane, interminable brown walls of the Louvre, punctuated by flamboyant towers and mansard roofs, fortunately were lost in the trees farther to the west. It is easy to empathize with Marie de Médicis, who grew tired of the Louvre and ordered the construction of Luxembourg Palace and Gardens, modeled after the Pitti Palace and Boboli Gardens in Florence.

Notre Dame

Far in the distance, atop a steeply rising hill to the north, we saw Sacré Coeur, overlooking the city and standing like a grand protector. Its soft white domes seemed to blend with the clouds, giving it an even greater lightness—so light that it appeared like a mirage floating above the simple housing of Montmartre, which followed the natural sloping contours of the hill. In the foreground to Montmartre, brilliant colors screamed with passion regardless of the weather. If not familiar with the Pompidou Center, one might think it just another building enveloped in scaffolding; yet in spite of its lack of elegance, the Pompidou has a magnetism and dynamism that wonderfully contrast with the gray and cream-colored stone walls often seen in this city. Closest to the river are the fantastic roofs of the Hôtel de Ville. On a sunny day, the roofs reflect a purple sheen, but as the clouds darkened so did the roofs, and all their color faded.

On my fourth Sunday in Paris, I finally arrived at Notre Dame in time for the 10:30 A.M. Mass, but before entering I was pleasantly distracted by the cries of a violin played by a middle-aged man standing in the shade of the southwest tower, within the Parvis. He was playing the Air from the Brandenburg Concerto no. 4, by Johann Sebastian Bach, with such intensity and passion that even the most aloof and rushing of the tourists were arrested in their steps for a moment. He played in perfect synchronization with the accompanying instruments sounding from his tape deck. In front of him was a violin case filled with silver coins and a picture of a young boy taped on the inside. Although the meaning of the picture remained obscure, the music evoked such a tragic nostalgia that even the coldest of souls could not help being affected.

The somber eloquence of the solitary violinist transcended the ridiculous circus atmosphere just north, where another crowd gathered around a donkey with hopes for family photos. Annoyed, I hastened to enter the cathedral. Inside, a soft euphony of music from the enormous organ echoed throughout the darkened nave, lit by the low morning sun through the tall leaded-glass windows, with shadows cast by the massive flying buttresses outside. Just as early morning mist rises from the earth in autumn, a haze of the familiar smell of incense lifted and permeated the church. The altar and priest were shrouded in this haze and surrounded by flickering candles. All rose as the Mass began. Though the service lacked a long sermon and failed to address seriously the political and cultural problems of our times, it fulfilled a need to worship for all those who attended. Though I did not comprehend most of the Gospel readings in French, the music spoke a universal language that I recalled from similar Catholic Masses in the United States. If indeed there is a language of the soul, this church understands and speaks it well.

Exiting to the riveting, exalting pounding of the organ, I again entered the Parvis Notre Dame, squinting at the sun-washed square filled by the masses. The violinist had moved in order to remain within the shadow of the cathedral, now facing the central portal, the typanum of which depicts Judgment Day. As before, passersby stopped at the sound, which dominated the air, filling it with a heaviness slowly filtered by the sun.

Walking away across Pont St. Louis toward Pont Louis Philippe, I remained entranced as I crossed the bridge to the Right Bank. There I came upon the magnificently picturesque view up the gentle cobblestone steps of Rue des Barres toward the mysterious Marais, where opulence coexists with squalor as in no other area in Paris.

To the east, beyond the southern garden of Notre Dame, across the Quai de l'Archevêché at the very end of the island, is the Mémorial de la Déportation, commemorating the two hundred thousand French who died during the Holocaust (thirty thousand from Paris alone). This memorial achieves a fine balance between abstract and literal symbolism. The literal is represented as an enclosed volume cut deep in the earth, with chambers reminiscent of prison cells branching off from an octagonal central space entered from a sunken courtyard of paved concrete open to the sky. The open court is surrounded by rough concrete walls that converge, stopping just short of a point and forming a narrow slit that reveals the Seine beyond. Here an abstract, black iron sculpture is suspended in front of this opening, through which the rippling, flowing river creates a haunting image suggestive of the freedom the prisoners could not achieve.

The stark simplicity of the design, built of concrete with embedded quartz pebbles (which represent the number of French who died during the Holocaust), appropriately conveys the magnitude and sense of loss. The solitude of the recessed monument allows visitors to mourn and contemplate in privacy, while the life of street performers, musicians, and the masses carries on with vigor and enthusiasm on the nearby Pont St. Louis. The physical confines of the memorial ended when we stepped from the last embedded quartz pebble onto the common paving of the bridge, but the haunting memory will always remain.

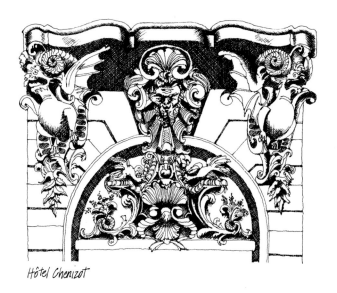

Hôtel Chenizot

East of the Ile de la Cité is the charming and provincial Ile St. Louis. Our day on this island was a pleasant surprise; the weather was sublime, the shops were exquisite, and automobile traffic was nearly nonexistent. Though a small island in comparison with the Ile de la Cité, it is incredibly rich in character and is home to many intact structures dating from the seventeenth century. The seventeenth-century architect Louis Le Vau resided here and designed many of the residences, otherwise known as *hôtels*, for aristocrats. We were not able to enter any of them, but after circling the island twice, my wife settled in front of the eighteenth-century Hôtel Chenizot and proceeded to draw the Rococo ornamented entrance, while I wandered farther down Rue St. Louis en l'Ile to Rue de Bretonvilliers. I, too, settled on a sidewalk to paint the street scene, which culminated with a three-story, mansard-roofed residence spanning Rue de Bretonvilliers. Early in the sketch the owner of the residence came out and seemed interested in what I was doing, but for fear of losing my concentration, I practically ignored the man. He never saw the final product, but perhaps it is just as well—though the drawing was acceptable, I'm sure he didn't fathom his house merely acceptable. Later I realized my foolishness; many of Paris's wealthy fashion designers, such as Yves St. Laurent, reside on this island. Perhaps someday I'll mail a copy of the finished product.

Ile St. Louis: Rue Brettonvilliers

# The Latin Quarter

*P*lace St. Michel is the gateway to the Latin Quarter. On a previous visit we had been so intent on changing money that I was hardly aware of the grand fountain that dominates the void. The blackened north face of the fountain of St. Michel fighting a dragon creates a backdrop for students, drifters, and drunks who loiter in anticipation of the next event, usually their wishes are granted and some sort of activity transpires. One late afternoon, Thai rock musicians performed numerous Dire Straits songs with great confidence and skill. Guitar riffs echoed from the surrounding walls as people danced and sang. Such activities blend with the constant buzzing of the automobiles that feed into the square from Boulevard St. Michel, Rue Danton, and Rue de la Harpe to drown the sound of the gushing fountain and diminish its artistic significance. Yet without the fountain, Place St. Michel would be simply another broad avenue.

Just south of Place St. Michel is the fourteenth-century Hôtel de Cluny, now a museum that straddles Roman baths from the second century. It is fascinating that buildings in Paris are often jammed together with

Hôtel Cluny

little or no respect for one another, yet the result is often magnificent, as at the Hôtel de Cluny. The great difference between the disjunctive relationships of the *hôtel* and the baths, as opposed to the colliding efforts evident in today's modern cities, is that the old mansion and baths are both load-bearing-wall buildings constructed of an indigenous stone material. Though different in style, their methods of construction and materials are nearly identical, as are their colors. In today's cities, the methods of construction are diverse; materials are abundant and widely available from anywhere, and there is virtually no limit to the height of buildings. Hence, rarely do we see contemporary buildings that are compatible, even when designed in seemingly similar styles. Perhaps in another four hundred years people will see them differently, though it is doubtful that many of today's buildings will still be standing.

Sketching within the southern courtyard at the Hôtel de Cluny was very challenging, though in a different way from most. In drawing Classical architecture, a trained architect can perceive elements of repetition, scale, and proportion through observation and education. At the medieval Cluny, however, there is little repetition, which necessitates the careful study of the relationships of all parts when drawing. The end result is a graceful and charming building, though a careful, rational analysis would point out many oddities. In many ways the medieval building is a more honest expression of its interior than the purely Classical building, which often is merely a formal facade concealing a more complicated interior.

While no building can epitomize the Gothic style, the Hôtel de Cluny is one of the few great examples of residential Gothic architecture in Paris that contrasts with the repetitive, classically inspired residences lining many streets of the city. While Classical architecture strives toward perfection, Gothic architecture reveals its imperfections, linking itself more closely to life and its potential flaws. Gothic architecture, as represented by the Hôtel de Cluny, is also more introverted than many other classically inspired buildings, but this is not simply a stylistic difference. Medieval Paris was rather unclean and in many ways unsafe, thus the residence was built around a courtyard protected by high crenellated stone walls, not unlike a medieval fortress. The residence does not address the life on the street nor the surrounding context; it is its own entity.

What is so appealing about buildings like the Hôtel de Cluny is their great vitality and implication of change. The architecture is not rigid or incapable of alteration; it can be added to or subtracted from without destroying the whole. The Hôtel de Cluny is picturesque, but not without any order or common architectural vocabulary. There are motifs and stylistic elements—pointed arches, crenellated stone walls, tracery within leaded-glass windows, bundled shafts—that tie together the informal ensemble to create a harmonious whole. The beauty in Gothic lies in its crudeness, its lack of predictability, but its dynamism can only be successful when incorporated within some order, for without order or rhythm, the dynamic becomes chaotic—it has no reference by which to measure its variation.

The Sorbonne, France's oldest and most prestigious university, looms just south of the Hôtel de Cluny, across a delightfully intimate park. In warmer months, the park is often full of older Parisians feeding birds and enjoying the shade from the hot summer sun. During my visit to the Sorbonne, a guard stood outside one of the entrances as professors and students passed through the monumental arched opening, which must first have appeared grand to them all, but from regularly and constantly passing through now serves merely as a practical gateway through which to enter and exit the university. Mounting the stairs and passing through the entrance, one looks down a long, classically inspired gallery with a thirty-foot-high, barrel-vaulted ceiling. On the left are frescoes painted within arched bays that support the vault. Completed in 1902, they depict magnificent monuments of the world: the temple at Philae in Egypt, Hagia Sophia in Istanbul, the Roman Forum, the Parthenon in Athens, and others. Each was done with impressive mastery and complete accuracy. Footsteps echo off the hard surfaces throughout the long gallery, which culminates in a great courtyard entirely paved in stone and surrounded by punctured yellow-stone walls. Within, framed by the court walls, is the university chapel designed by Jacques Lemercier, completed in 1642. It is the sole building remaining from the time of Cardinal Richelieu, who was the grand master in the seventeenth century and commissioned Lemercier to restore the dilapidated college buildings and design a Jesuit-style church. Stairs

Sorbonne Chapel

lead up to the Baroque-inspired church, with a statue of Victor Hugo at the base of the steps to the left and one of Louis Pasteur to the right— men of the arts and sciences preceding and flanking the spiritual world beyond.

In great contrast with the humble, stuccoed walls and narrow streets that characterize the residential area of the Latin Quarter are the church at the Sorbonne and the Panthéon—both powerful and sure, pure and architectonic. The domes and surrounding squares of these monuments provide foci to the meandering, picturesque streets of the Left Bank. During the summer, the Place de la Sorbonne is quiet, and few visitors frequent the cafés that neighbor the bookstores; but in September the character becomes vastly different. The cafés are full of students and professors who sit for hours over a single cup of coffee. Groups converse, while individuals bury their heads in books, oblivious to the surrounding sounds and activities. Student musicians perform classical music for menial patronage, while vagabonds peacefully sleep on nearby benches.

The incoming freshmen seemed more focused on initiation rites and various traditional ceremonies than on their studies. One day a group of young students dressed in medieval garb with black ink stamps smeared on their foreheads and cheeks were carrying torn pages from old texts, selling them to individuals on the street for any sum of money. While they wandered the streets in search of sponsors, the oblivious loners still sat at the surrounding cafés, scarcely looking up from their texts, and other groups continued to converse about their summer experiences and the upcoming school year. September in Paris is like a new year. Most Parisians are back from vacation, students begin school, and a revivified enthusiasm is evident everywhere.

Farther south is the center of the Latin Quarter, where the eighteenth-century Panthéon rests. Like all of Paris's great monuments, the Panthéon soars above all that surrounds it. There is no confusion as to its importance in shaping the physical environment, nor to its place in history. Originally conceived by Jacques-Germain Soufflot in 1755 as a temple honoring Ste. Geneviève, the patron saint of Paris, it now stands as a monument to the many great French people who died during the period of French liberty. It also houses the tombs of other great men of various distinctive backgrounds in France's history. Though the Panthéon is a rather awkward and unfriendly edifice, from afar the copper dome and cupola resting on the simply punctured circular stone wall that surmounts a broader ring of columns form a pure, simple, and easily grasped image. It conveys a rational strength and stability at the heart of Paris's intellectual center. Perched atop a gently rising hill, the Panthéon rests within a generous square open to Rue Soufflot, which aligns with the nearby Luxembourg Gardens and the distant Eiffel Tower to the west.

After returning from Italy in 1755, Soufflot spent the remainder of his life working on the Pantheon. There are obvious references to the ancient Pantheon in Rome, but Soufflot was seeking not only a pure and monumental architecture, but also one that would achieve the lightness of the Gothic. One way Soufflot tried to achieve this lightness was by designing the great central dome to be supported simply by columns, similar to that of Hagia Sophia; but after three decades of constant structural failures and financial woes, Soufflot went mad with frustration, which led to severe depression and ultimately his suicide. In the end, the Panthéon was completed by his student Rondelet in 1789, and the dome was supported by massive stone piers.

While many of Soufflot's positive design ideas are still evident, there is a mournfulness about the present condition of the Panthéon, especially when viewed from the street. But during Paris's long summer sunsets the Panthéon is particularly powerful. It seems to stand and sit simultaneously, looking comfortably out past the Luxembourg Gardens to the soaring frame of cast iron silhouetted against the setting sun. As the great golden light washes the Panthéon's grand portico, the words commemorating the people who died, carved in gold in its tympanum, shimmer with reflections, as if reminding one of the crypt below where Voltaire, Hugo, and others rest in peace. The Panthéon is strong, yet it is wounded. It somehow wants to reach out and pull you up to its heavenly temple near the clouds, but its massive walls at the street level stare blankly, and the scars still show from the Constituent Assembly's ordering of the blocking of the forty-two windows for fear of further violent destruction during the

Panthéon

Revolution. From a distance, its blemishes are no longer regarded, however; its purity shines and carries forth the strength that Soufflot envisioned and sadly never realized.

When we visited Paris two years before, the Panthéon had distracted us from exploring two wonderful and significant adjacent monuments. The first is the nineteenth-century Bibliothèque Ste. Geneviève by Henri Labrouste. This remarkable stone-and-iron library was revolutionary in comparison with contemporary works, but less mature than Labrouste's later Bibliothèque Nationale on the Right Bank; still, it was an epoch-making building. While it is noted most often for its technical innovation, it is a much more sophisticated building that can be read on many levels. Labrouste, like many other architects of his time, traveled to Italy to study the ancient Roman ruins in 1824, but he rejected the common search for the ideal form of architecture in antiquity; he interpreted the ancient architecture as being much more unpredictable and, perhaps more important, re-created the ancient temples with enormous measured ink drawings, richly decorating the buildings with color. Because of this radical view of antiquity, Labrouste was ostracized and didn't receive any commissions for many years after his return from Italy, but finally, in 1840, Labrouste won the commission for Bibliothèque Ste. Geneviève.

Much of what he had learned in Italy is evident in the library's utter simplicity and Classical proportions, but in addition to bringing the past to the present via architecture, he also respected the great potential of new materials and other industrial innovations. The Bibliothèque Ste. Geneviève is not only the first artificially lit library, it is also one of the first major buildings other than greenhouses, market halls, and train stations to incorporate iron as a major structural material. Exposed iron trusses thrust upon a central row of columns to create a double nave and a vast open public space. The iron is not simply structural, though; it is quite decorative, bearing motifs that are incorporated into other parts of the building. What results is a remarkable balance of function, the antique, and new technology — one concept does not overwhelm the other.

The exterior of the library is rather static and ominous, but it is almost modern in the way it reflects the interior functions on the outside. The lower story is minimally punctured with tall, narrow arched windows; this was done not only for security reasons, but also to express the subsidiary functions of the lower levels. The two-story library and reading space is expressed by repetitive, two-story arched openings infilled with engraved stone panels nearly half the height of the two-storied arches. The incised panels bear the names of authors whose books lie directly behind.

It is this literal symbolism as well as crafted detailing and ornament that prevent the Bibliothèque Ste. Geneviève from being a long, monotonous, rectangular building. Labrouste believed strongly that simple, carefully detailed rectangular structures, not unlike ancient Greek temples, could be just as, or perhaps more so than, interesting structures with many interlocking volumes and masses. This theory certainly works at the Bibliothèque Ste. Geneviève.

The other building we neglected before is a remarkably eclectic church east of the Panthéon called St. Etienne du Mont. This church sits picturesquely at the top of the winding Rue de la Montagne Ste. Geneviève. In striking contrast with the ancient Roman-inspired geometric purity of the Panthéon, St. Etienne is a conglomeration of numerous styles. Baroque, Classical, Gothic, and even Byzantine influences are seen when one wanders about the church. This is a result both of its having been designed eclectically and of its having been built over a period of centuries. Smaller structures are attached outside with steeply pitched mansard roofs and a variety of projections; yet these humbly simple and awkward additions complement and add romance to the already picturesque ensemble. As with the Hôtel de Cluny, it is difficult to grasp any pure image of St. Etienne, but impossible to forget its narrow Gothic tower soaring above the stepped-back masses of walls and roofs. Looking up Rue de la Montagne, St. Etienne's bell tower appears slightly skewed toward Place du Panthéon, where one is shocked by the severity of the blank stone walls of the Panthéon, which stands nearly as tall as the tower itself.

■　　■　　■

St. Etienne du Mont

*St. Etienne du Mont*

South of the heart of the Latin Quarter is the Tour Montparnasse—a modern high rise that, oddly, soars alone, above all else. It marks the district where many United States and European expatriate literary figures from the 1920s congregated, especially on the grand Boulevard du Montparnasse. The boulevard is loaded with cafés and bookstores as it has always been, but today enormous movie houses line the street as well. Americans frequent the famous cafés, which no longer offer "cheap American breakfasts" as they did during the twenties and thirties to such writers as Ernest

Hemingway, Henry Miller, and e. e. cummings; Rotonde, Dôme, La Coupole, and Sélect all remain, but their clientele has greatly changed. La Coupole has become very fashionable after an expensive renovation, and in the evenings promises to offer a riveting time with numerous people dancing well into the night. My visit to La Coupole was limited to a *café-crème* on a Thursday morning when only a handful of tourists sat on the terrace in deference to its literary past. All that remains of the original character are the twelve columns painted by such artists as Chagall, Léger, and Brancusi. After finishing my *café* and paying homage to the great literary figures of the past, I leisurely headed east toward yet another of Paris's markers—the church of Val de Grâce—to find the towering Baroque dome designed by François Mansart.

Most of the buildings on Boulevard du Montparnasse are seven stories high with mansard roofs. They are all stone, but lack the elaborate ornament of those on the Right Bank. Trees line the street, as they do all the major boulevards in Paris, their trunks rising just above the glassed-in terraces that compose the buildings' street level, in contrast with the open cafés in the city center.

At the intersection with Boulevard St. Michel and the terminus of the Luxembourg Gardens is the Port Royal, where the character of the boulevard abruptly changes. One's view is no longer linearly directed, but instead is treated to the great vistas to the north and east. To the north, the Luxembourg Palace is revealed through a mass of heavily foliaged trees, and to the east, a conglomeration of vernacular architecture of painted stucco apartments and stone monuments marks the Latin Quarter.

Once off the boulevard one experiences almost utter silence, except for the bells of the churches, which ring every half hour. In front of the Val de Grâce church, which was designed by François Mansart and Jacques Lemercier and built between 1645 and 1667, the square was empty except for two tourists who were gazing up at the flamboyant, heavily ribbed dome, which rests upon a series of buttresses in the form of Corinthian pilasters. This dynamic church is very much like the one at the Invalides, though it is not at the terminus of any great axis; it is nestled within a densely populated neighborhood and is hardly visible except from atop the various monuments that speckle Paris. The nearby Panthéon is stark and stoic in comparison with this church, but the dynamism of Val de Grâce is unanswered by the emptiness and silence of the nearby streets, while the blank walls of the Panthéon are enlivened by the colorful masses of people who continually grace its surrounding square.

Unlike the great Gothic cathedrals of Paris, the Baroque Val de Grâce church displays very little emphasis on procession. All attention is focused on the center, which is surmounted by the dominant dome. The interior of the dome appears weightless through the masterful painting, depicting heavenly life and stories from the Bible. Frescoes for Baroque cathedrals required clear light to be seen; thus, the use of stained-glass windows typical of Gothic cathedrals gave way to clear glass, and these paintings became the principal source for the teachings to the people. The church's refined purity is indicative of the profound influence of the Italian Renaissance on France, but perhaps in its learned intellectual precision it fails to evoke the enchantment and spiritual illumination of the Gothic cathedrals manifest throughout Paris.

After meandering along Rue Lhomond onto Rue du Pot de Fer just north of Val de Grâce, I found my way back to the colorful, narrow, and sloping Rue Mouffetard. A walk in the Latin Quarter would not be complete without visiting this street. The buildings are mostly stucco with very little ornament. They rarely parallel the street and occasionally are set far enough back to allow pushcarts to set up small markets. Also, at certain points the sidewalk widens and accommodates wooden, covered sheds at which are sold fresh-cooked crepes and baguette sandwiches at one-third the price of restaurants. The odors and sounds on Rue Mouffetard are rich and numerous, especially during lunch hour, but before and after lunch one hears the constant pounding of hammers and the murmuring of saws from behind the walls, as this area is in a constant state of restoration.

At the base of the slope and southern end of the street is an African/Brazilian market, with an assortment of exotic fruits and vegetables, bordering a more traditional market at the intersection with Rue Monge. Next to a butcher's store, where multiple cow and pig heads are displayed in the storefront, a famous brasserie marks the entrance to the market. Diagonally across the street is a *pâtisserie* full of wonderful tarts, croissants, and various other breads sculpted into humorous shapes. Late in the afternoon, people returning home from work shop here for their evening meals or for snacks. A few hints of cobblestones are visible under the mostly new asphalt paving, but the stone street curbs remain nearly one foot high, recalling an earlier time when sewage must have flowed freely down the roadside gutters. Most of the walls and storefronts have been repainted, but some aged storefronts of blackened timber are seen intermittently. The narrow street gently turns so that one never has a clear vista up the richly colored road full of signs, canopies, and pushcarts, all projecting from the modest buildings of various hues and simple fenestrations.

At Place de la Contrescarpe the street name changes to Rue Descartes, and the character changes as well, as restaurants dominate the street life. The narrow Rue Mouffetard opens onto this square that is hardly beautiful; no fountain or monument graces the center, and the central island has no grass but is paved in asphalt, from which rise cast-iron light poles and a few isolated and misplaced trees. But the cafés and restaurants, which define the perimeter, add richness with pedestrian life, colors, and smells that distinguish the square from other ordinary intersections and the nearby streets with their four-storied residences that otherwise go unnoticed.

Hemingway referred to Place de la Contrescarpe with great affection in "The Snows of Kilimanjaro." He resided near the square in the twenties and recalled the working people who all knew one another. At that time the houses had white plastered walls above, with brown at the street level; still today, the oddly tilted walls, finished in painted plaster, are only a little more brown from age and pollution. The restaurants are still comparatively inexpensive, but as one begins the descent from Place de la Contrescarpe (on Rue Descartes or Rue du Cardinal Lemoine) toward the banks of the Seine, the restaurant prices rise, though the difference may only be in the table setting. Brightly colored paper table covers and dulled glass and flatware are replaced by tables set with silver and crystal upon white linen tablecloths.

Farther east, up a secluded hill and surrounded by trees, is one of Paris's most important Roman ruins—Arènes de Lutèce, from the late second century. The large oval amphitheater, surrounded by stone seating that once could hold ten thousand spectators, is now only a stage where older Frenchmen compete in *boules,* and young French boys play soccer with their goals at either end of the main theater entrances. The centrally focused, bowl-shaped space provides a tranquil and entertaining divergence from the linear streets, which sometimes seem directionless and interminable. It also responds beautifully to the natural landscape, as it is built into the sloping earth. Away from the populace, the ageless arena is an entertaining place to have a picnic and watch people. The arena still exists thanks to its relatively recent discovery in 1869, and it gracefully ages with the surrounding trees and earth, living in peace, seemingly remote yet within the bustle of the city.

Farther east of the Roman arena is the Jardin des Plantes in Paris's Islamic quarter. Bordering these botanical gardens, a large, tile-glazed mosque with soaring minarets is surrounded by a ten-foot-high wall that dominates the neighborhood. On Fridays—the Islamic holy day—Muslims dressed in white traverse the gardens to the gates of the mosque to pray to Allah.

Within the Jardin des Plantes is the Paris zoo and a number of museums that run parallel to the formal gardens to the south. Along the southern edge of the park are three galleries comprising the Museums of Natural History. The most architecturally interesting of these is the Musée Paléontologique—a long magnificent structure of stone, iron, and brick, designed in the late nineteenth century by C. L. F. Dutert, the architect of the Palais des Machines (now destroyed) for the 1889 Exposition. Beyond the lobby, a grand, two-story space rises fifty feet and is covered by a flat, glass-gridded ceiling that floats below the structure above. Most striking are the ornamental metalwork and the iron structure. The rails and balustrades are elaborate manifestations of plants and nature, swirling and twisting in a repetitive motif that synchronizes with the skeletons of mammoth reptiles and dinosaurs. The ornamental snakes entwine with the balusters at the base of the stairs that lead to a cantilevered mezzanine overlooking the entire exhibit. It is disturbing that the Palais des Machines was destroyed, but at least this museum remains as a suggestion of what must have been a remarkable building.

The Jardin des Plantes is a pleasant park designed in the early seventeenth century as a royal herb garden. As at the Palais Royal, double rows of manicured lime trees border the long rectangular space, providing an isolating buffer from the museums to the south and the zoo to the north. The enormous garden is beautifully maintained and is a wonderful place to promenade and enjoy a vast array of colors and scents that provide respite from the gray and cream-colored walls defining the surrounding streets.

Just northwest of the Jardin des Plantes, bordering the Seine, is the Institut du Monde Arabe—one of François Mitterrand's pet projects from the 1980s. Designed by Jean Nouvel, the institute is more like a monument than a museum. The design is spatially quite inefficient, with vertical circulation taking up one-third of the area, and horizontal circulation another twenty-five percent, leaving only forty percent usable space. Nonetheless, it is an impressive structure with remarkable architectural details and connections that transform the very ordinary materials of aluminum and glass. The most notable and memorable aspect of the building is the grid of screens covering the entire south facade. These extraordinary mechanically and visually intricate screens electronically operate from photovoltaic sensors to regulate the amount of sunlight penetrating the all-glass facade. Although highly sophisticated in their technology, they are reminiscent of the elaborate stone screens of Islamic architecture. It is unlikely that the mechanical screens can outlast the ancient stone screens, which require little maintenance, though they are effective in many similar ways. Inside, they control the infiltration of natural light, while also casting shadows in ornamental patterns on the simple concrete floors, bringing to mind decorative Persian carpets. The screens are also reflected in the many interior glass walls, multiplying their presence and creating disorienting abstract images.

The exterior skin reflects the changing light intensity, not unlike

Notre Dame
from Left Bank

The Latin Quarter from Ile St. Louis

the way a chameleon changes colors. As the sun intensifies, the screens close and the wall becomes more reflective of the surrounding environment and the sky. When the screens open, the building reads like a single, simple mass, but the elements of texture and pattern of the punctured screens underlie the entire reflection. In addition to its unique architectural character, the institute also has a rooftop pavilion and restaurant. Situated at the southeast bend of the Seine, magnificent views over Paris make the institute worth the sojourn even more.

Bordering the institute is Quai de la Tournelle. Numerous restaurants line the southern side of this particular stretch, while card and poster entrepreneurs hawk their various journals and etchings on the side bordering the Seine. At the midpoint of the *quai* is the famous restaurant La Tour d'Argent. Because we weren't very hungry we opted to visit the restaurant gift shop instead, where we were warmly greeted by the shopkeeper. Rudimentary phrases were spoken in French and the more complicated in English, but she applauded our attempts nonetheless and left us with a menu so that we could be prepared when we return in twenty years.

The *quais* of the Latin Quarter are also graced by a quaint park called Square René Viviani, adjacent to the humble church St. Julien le Pauvre, noted by some to be the oldest church in Paris. (It was started after Notre Dame but completed earlier.) Sloping lawns, scattered with ruins from Notre Dame, encircle a paved plaza with a modest fountain in the center. It is an enjoyable place to picnic, warmed by the sun and cooled by refreshing breezes from the nearby Seine, with the ever-present Notre Dame looming beyond, through and above the trees.

West of the park and north of the Seine is a labyrinth of streets where inexpensive restaurants abound. On the Rue de la Huchette, the Rue St. Séverin, and Rue de la Harpe, the smells are unmistakable. The heavy aromas of French fries, gyros, and souvlakia seem to have saturated the damp walls that define the streets.

François Mitterrand also resides in this area, on Rue de Bièvre, a narrow street just south of Pont de l'Archevêché and perpendicular to the Seine. His house appears quite large, but is minimally adorned, except for the wild ivy that grows freely upon the stucco walls. The humble style and intimate integration into the city fabric of Mitterrand's house are in great contrast with the White House in Washington, which stands as a singular building within a highly restricted garden of trees, flowers, and grass. The White House is a Classical villa within the urban landscape, isolated and proud. Mitterrand's house is an extension of the vernacular urban context. If not for the guards stationed at either end of the street, one would never distinguish Mitterrand's house from its neighbors.

# St. Germain

*I*n the gentrified area that extends from the Musée d'Orsay east to Place St. Michel, bordering Boulevard St. Germain, charming, elegant stores have replaced the artisans' shops and light-manufacturing quarters that previously presided there. Still, having never explored the area in its more innocent times, I found it to contain a fine balance, representative of all types of people and architecture.

At the western terminus of Boulevard St. Germain is the now-famous Musée d'Orsay. We only gazed at the museum (once a train station) from the outside, admiring its grand and powerful presence and sweeping Art Nouveau–inspired, steel-and-glass canopy. For most, the art inside is the allure of the Musée d'Orsay, but I decided to return at another time when the sun was not shining so brightly and the crowds were less dense.

When I first visited the museum in 1989, only three years after its opening, I found it to be tremendous, metaphorically linking the ancient and Renaissance art from the Louvre to the modern art in the Pompidou Center. It is a perfectly appropriate structure to house nineteenth-century art. Designed during the late nineteenth century, the building represents a time when industrialization and socialism had powerful influences on art and culture. The late nineteenth century also ended the era of Romanticism and marked the beginning of modern art, which this building certainly reflects as well. Its mass-produced, repetitive ordering of steel and glass, combined with its ornate, coffered, barrel-vaulted ceiling, evoke an appearance that is at once tectonic and decorative.

A rail company bought the site in 1871, after a palace was devastated by fire, and commissioned Victor Laloux to design a train station, which was completed in 1900. The building took less than two years of continuous, around-the-clock construction by three hundred men. In the 1930s, with the development of longer trains, which increasingly were being powered by electricity, the station became defunct. It served various functions until 1961, when it was almost destroyed. Le Corbusier was one of many architects who supported its demolition, and he proposed an 870-room hotel to replace it. Thousands of people signed a petition to prevent this, and finally in the early 1970s the station was declared a historic landmark. The exterior and much of the interior were restored to reflect its original character (without the railroad tracks), and the museum design was done by a prominent Italian designer, Gae Aulenti.

The renovation is a fairly successful balance of maintaining the museum's oddly contrasting overwrought ornamentalism with its industrial nature of steel and glass, but the infilled forms by Aulenti seem out of place and temporary, perhaps due to their simple and massive forms and their allusions to load-bearing construction, but this, too, might be perfectly appropriate considering the power and permanence of the original structure.

The exterior is fabulous in its dichotomous monumentality and steel-and-glass tracery. Its grand scale speaks of its importance, but the use of delicate and elaborate steel and glass gives the building a less foreboding, more inviting character. Again, there is the tremendous balance of purity and intricacy so prevalent in France's late-nineteenth- and early-twentieth-century architecture.

Just east of the museum, perpendicular to the Seine, is a charming street called Rue du Bac, named after the ferries (*bacs*) that once transported quarry stone across the Seine. Today, Rue du Bac is not nearly so functional but full of amusing shops, restaurants, and galleries. To the north it aligns with the terminal pavilion that marks the end of the Louvre (something I did not think I would ever find), and to the south, Rue du Bac intersects Boulevard St. Germain and extends into a quiet residential area where many French diplomats live, including France's prime minister, Jacques Chirac, who lives at Hôtel Matignon.

This quiet and privileged residential area is effectively divided by Boulevard Raspail, yet another slice through Paris that runs north and south. To the east of the tree-lined boulevard, numerous streets intersect at acute angles and are lined with very elegant shops intended for the upper-middle-class Parisians. Each small shop is unique, built in scale with the existing neighborhood fabric. The buildings combine eclectic and interesting mixes of eighteenth-, nineteenth-, and twentieth-century styles. Some are clad in stucco with simple painted wooden shutters; others are grand and ornate, celebrating the multiple intersections with slate-tiled domed roofs surmounting elaborately carved stone cornices. Stone frames define the tall French windows that open out to intimate, undulating balconies of wrought iron, the ornate delicacy of which contrasts with the strong horizontal and vertical lines of the walls.

In this area, one can find Poilâne, a world-famous bakery run by Lionel Poilâne. The bread baked here is served at some four hundred restaurants in Paris and is flown daily to gourmet shops from New York to Tokyo. I can only imagine that the stores in New York and Tokyo must vary greatly from the original—a very small and unpretentious shop with a single employee in a white smock greeting and serving those who frequent the place. If not for the extraordinary display of breads in the storefront windows, and the exorbitant prices listed below, this store might go unnoticed altogether.

Nestled within a residential neighborhood to the east of Boulevard Raspail is the enormous church of St. Sulpice, which we approached from the rear. The sun illuminated the top of this magnificent church, while the tall colonnade of the north facade, with its pedimented side entrance, retreated in shadow. The neighboring buildings rise barely to the

St. Sulpice

second tier of the grand edifice, but still stand close enough to the church walls so that the magnitude of the church is perceived. From the large, open square before the front facade, tricks of Classical proportions that create illusions of scale can be appreciated. The horizontal ordering comprises only two levels, and when viewed from a distance in the square, it appears modest and not at all overwhelming. Yet when one stands directly adjacent to the building's massive walls and columns, its monumental ordering and scale become apparent.

St. Sulpice

The front elevation was a disappointment after I first saw the dynamic rear of the church, where richness and complexity abound. The front is severe and staid and not very ecclesiastical looking, excepting the mismatched bell towers, whose difference in design resulted not only from shifting sands under the foundation, but also from indecision on the part of the church patrons. The church was designed and built over a span of one hundred and forty-three years (1645–1788), which at least partially explains its odd appearance, but the front facade was designed primarily by the Italian theater and stage designer Giovanni Servandoni in 1732, some say in defiance of its Rococo and Baroque interior. However, the interior of the church is more cohesive, though it, too, appears to be unfinished conceptually. Still, like the many marvelous Renaissance cathedrals in Italy, there are fantastic paintings in the side chapels by famous French artists of the time, such as Eugène Delacroix and Jean-Baptiste Pigalle, and a striking sculpture in the Lady Chapel at the rear of the church. But the prodigious organ, designed by Chalgrin in 1776, on the upper level at the front of the nave is the work of art that dominates the interior. It is one of the largest organs in the world.

Interior: St. Sulpice

After viewing the interior, I again circled the exterior and found myself at the southeast corner near the rear of the church, where the caretaker's structure abuts the cathedral. It was quiet except for a few men who drank wine feverishly in the sun, listening to soccer with uninhibited enthusiasm. The life of hedonism so close to the confines of the church seemed entirely paradoxical, but then I remembered reading about the lavish banquet for 1,200 people this church hosted after Napoléon's victories in Egypt, and I realized how harmless the soccer-and-wine enthusiasts were in comparison.

Toward the close of summer on a late Sunday afternoon, under a gorgeous blue sky, the Luxembourg Palace and Gardens could be mistaken for an earthly paradise. The diverse, wonderful gardens were appropriately full of Parisians enjoying what was perhaps the last Sunday of summer before vacations were to end. Men and women sat in the shade at the Fontaine de Médicis, where the statues of a pair of young, nude lovers embrace below the ominous bronze sculpture of the massive Polyphemus. North of the fountain, singles, couples, and families sat outside a pavilion, sipping tea or coffee, or perhaps eating lavish ice-cream dishes. Canopied under the large trees, which filtered spots of light, the scene was reminiscent of a French Impressionist painting. Young boys and girls raced toy sailboats in the large central basin as their parents basked in the sun. Farther east, children rode ponies down a dusty dirt road that ran between the popular and completely full tennis and basketball courts.

While some people came to watch, others came to play. But on a Sunday, when all wished the sun would never set, there was something for everyone to do at the Luxembourg Gardens. The gardens do not function now as Marie de Médicis intended; neither do they adhere to Baron Haussmann's grand plans. But today they give pleasure and peace to those who desire tranquillity, and an outlet to those who seek activity. In 1615 Marie de Médicis hired the architect Salomon de Brosse to design a new palace in place of the Louvre. Her reasons were that she had grown tired of the Louvre and also needed a place to escape from the memory of the tragic death of her husband, Henri IV. Marie also wanted the palace to recall the character of the Pitti Palace in Florence. She got a few of her wishes, but the final design was more French in spirit in that it was placed between a courtyard and garden and screened from the main road. The greatest irony about the palace, however, was that Marie had been banished from Paris by her own son for turning against Cardinal Richelieu by the time the palace was finally completed in 1631.

Under the rule of Napoléon III in the mid-nineteenth century, Baron Haussmann did much to alter the character of Paris forever, but his plans to develop the sixty acres that compose the Luxembourg Gardens were vetoed by twelve thousand Parisians who signed a petition to save the park. This is most fortunate, because the Luxembourg Gardens, like Central Park in New York, are essential to the Parisians' way of life. As long as there is Paris, the gardens will always be part of it.

Walking north from the gardens toward the Seine (a familiar procedure), we encountered the venerable church of St. Germain des Prés. A powerful Benedictine abbey existed here for many centuries within an open pasture (hence the name "des Prés"), but after numerous additions, battles, urban plans, and other transforming events, only the church remains. The oldest sections of the church date back to the eleventh century, but the subsequent additions and renovations date from the twelfth to the nineteenth centuries. Sadly it has not withstood the test of time nearly so well as the seemingly ageless Notre Dame and Ste. Chapelle. The battered, fragmented structure is perhaps symbolic of its difficult past. In an adjacent court that once served as a cemetery a horrible massacre took place in 1792 when numerous monks and priests were hacked to death by an angry mob for siding with Paris's aristocrats. While many of Paris's buildings still stand boldly and elegantly, this church — which once stood within a magnificent enclave, surrounded by powerful fortifications — rests awkwardly out of place, seemingly ready to crumble and, ironically, to become yet another romantic ruin.

There are few open areas or urban parks between the Luxembourg Gardens and the Seine on the Left Bank, but adjacent to the church is a small playground where children were playing under the more or less watchful gazes of their mothers. While most cooperated and socialized

St. Germain des Prés

peacefully, one child's bullying tainted the otherwise harmonious occasion. This incident was certainly insignificant in comparison with the shameful and bloody mass executions that occurred here in the massacre of 1792, which it brought to mind.

Adjacent to the playground an artist/poet was working, unaffected by the energetic fervor of the noisy children. His work was hanging on the cast-iron fence separating the church from the street. In its color and vibrancy, it was unaffected by the history of St. Germain and offered poetry to those who passed. I later learned that the artist was one of many to display work at this site as part of a government-sponsored program supporting ethnic artists.

A bronze bust of Apollinaire, by Picasso, graces the northeast grounds of the church in another small park. Older people generally sit in peace and solitude on the few surrounding benches, feeding the pigeons as part of their daily routine. Today, the grounds of St. Germain des Prés are a haven of civility. But regardless of its present-day refinement, the cicatrices in the surface of the walls and the darkening of its tower from age and pollution are symbolic of St. Germain des Prés's tortured past. Sometimes crooked and cracked stone walls evoke images of romance, but not here.

Farther north of St. Germain des Prés, on Rue Bonaparte, is the once-prodigious Ecole des Beaux Arts. A wrought-iron gate surrounds this Neoclassical complex of buildings, which appear devoid of human activity. During the nineteenth century, the *école* was a world center of architectural education, and many famous American architects studied in its atelier system. Though ideological controversy often pervaded the school, the onslaught of Modernism reduced its

Ecole des Beaux Arts

importance, and it closed in 1968. It has reopened recently, but hardly attracts the attention it received in the nineteenth and early twentieth centuries. While French architects seemed to apply this Neoclassical training literally, such American graduates as Richard Morris Hunt, Henry Hobson Richardson, and Richard Maybeck used their training as groundwork for their own unique architectural expressions. One can see an obvious Neoclassical influence in their work, yet their buildings seem to be more inventive and personal than those of their French contemporaries. Being in America, away from the profound influence of the *école*, made it easier to form more personal interpretations. One can see this in much of Richardson's work in and around Boston. Furthermore, such American architects as Richardson and Hunt were also trying to create a new American architecture at that time. This may have also contributed to their looser interpretations of Classical architecture.

East of the *école*, on the Rue de Seine, Rue Visconti, and Rue des Beaux Arts, are many of Paris's contemporary art galleries. Only the poster and print shops ever appeared to have more than a few people in them, but like the Soho galleries in New York City, they represent the diverse and complex world of today's art. Like modern music, film, literature, and other media, much of the work focuses on sex and/or the body. This theme is hardly ephemeral, but seems rather to have evolved naturally over time. Given the changing artistic and conservative cultural tendencies of today, I wonder at the future significance of the human figure as a subject for art. However, for centuries it has served as an inspiration to artists and others, and it is unlikely that a momentary cultural conservatism will alter the importance of the human form in art.

At the heart of this artistic center are numerous cafés, none of which is frequented more than La Palette. Writers, artists, and other bohemians often meet throughout the day, particularly in the late afternoon before the galleries' opening receptions. La Palette is a rather large café that expands over a grand terrace and, amazingly, is serviced by only one waiter, who tends to matters quite efficiently, but with very little patience.

In the near distance, to the north, is a vibrant street market exhibiting the normal procedures of everyday life. The aromas of fresh-baked bread and colorful fruits and flowers smother the smell of oil paint from the nearby art galleries. The galleries breathe life, but with a unique energy and vigor, often shrouded by the proper behavior such places elicit. The market is a work of art as well, but contrary to the pieces displayed in the galleries, the market is in constant motion, engaging many aspects of life. We watched while parents sought the daily necessities, carrying baskets with fresh groceries in one hand and warm baguettes in the other; their children followed obediently, occasionally distracted by a musician who sang and played the accordion. He could often be found singing throughout the market in a deep, bellowing voice that was hardly remarkable, but added a simple charm to this natural, unforced environment.

In contrast with the loud and active streets of the market, and the haughty galleries nearby, is the peaceful, unpretentious, almost-hidden treasure of Place de Furstemberg. It is a short walk from St. Germain des Prés. Within the court, various shops sell antiques, textiles, sewing paraphernalia, and other crafts. Also, there is a small archway on the western facade leading to a very simple court, where one can find Eugène Delacroix's atelier. In the center of Place de Furstemberg is a lamppost on a square stone base where artists sometimes sit and meditate or solo musicians play amid four mature trees, which absorb the sounds just enough to enhance the euphony otherwise unhindered by the surrounding masonry walls. When there is no music, the only sounds are footsteps and the faint rustling of leaves, different from the usual rattling automobile engines heard on the busy neighboring streets. Though few bike riders brave the streets of Paris, an occasional rider may pass through the square but then quickly disappear into the lively, dense urban environment.

Like Place and Rue de Furstemberg, the nearby Rue de l'Abbaye defies the modern city. It is barely wide enough for an automobile to squeeze between the parked cars, which are rarely moved for fear of losing the precious parking spot. Rather than promenading along the walkways, people walk in the middle of the street, often with their miniature dogs on leashes or, sometimes, with their cats luxuriously and peacefully riding upon their shoulders. Perpendicular to Rue de l'Abbaye is Rue de l'Echaudé, another street where pedestrians take precedence. Again, it is constricted and slices through dense, simple buildings that have tiny window openings and low doorways at the street level. At the intersection with Rue de Seine, the atmosphere changes, though an element of peace still remains. The street opens up to the vast sky, and the sun, on clear days, washes the exterior facades near the top two stories, while the lower levels rest in shade.

The busier streets of Rue Danton and Rue St. André des Arts intersect to the west of Boulevard St. Michel. Here a small square marks the border between the student life of the Latin Quarter and the consumer world of St. Germain. The shops, neither elaborate nor posh, are simple and cluttered with an assortment of goods, ranging from clothes and furniture to books and jewelry.

Rue St. André des Arts, a narrow street with little traffic, offers wonderful glimpses down the many cross streets, spilling into the *quais* to the north and Place de l'Odéon and the Palais du Luxembourg to the south. The buildings are modest, and, in typical Parisian style, numerous small eclectic shops occupy the street level, their displays showing very little pretension. The balustrades on the upper floors are simple and purely functional; the walls are not elegant. Looking through the windows one senses an unpretentious interior character. We walked by the building in which e. e. cummings lived, and another where Jack Kerouac passed his time. Gertrude Stein and Alice Toklas resided just to the north on Rue Christine, after having been evicted from their previous apartment. While those who dwell in and roam this area today have changed, it still exudes an atmosphere of freedom.

Off Rue St. André des Arts, just east of Rue de Buci, is the Cour du Commerce St. André — the oldest covered passageway in Paris. Unlike the many elegantly designed arcades on the Right Bank near the Bibliothèque Nationale, the Cour du Commerce St. André, though planned, appears to be the result of urban accretion. The strictly utilitarian, glazed, pedimented roof rests unnaturally on the tilting one-and-a-half-story walls on either side. The space is both indoor and outdoor; it has none of the polished interior finishes of the Right Bank galleries, such as *faux* marble, mosaic flooring, or fancy light sconces. A narrow road of cobblestones

Institut de France

sunk deeply near the curb defines the narrow walk. Restaurants, bistros, and galleries line the passageway as they did in the eighteenth century, when the Cour du Commerce St. André was Paris's first covered shopping street. Over the low-rising, one-and-a-half-story buildings, the sunlight pours into this unsophisticated but charming alley and accents the vast array of colors that meld in the walls, signs, and flowers. The colors and the flickering, brilliant light cause the eye to wander, never allowing it to focus. While much of central Paris changed contemporaneously, reflecting its growing wealth, this passageway remains as a small reminder of Paris's past character. Baron Haussmann would hardly have approved of such vernacular eclecticism, but today it is an odd, but most welcome, diversion from the sometimes too-refined streets of Paris.

As one moves from the world of the market at Rue de Buci and Cour du Commerce St. André, progressing east toward Place St. Michel, the shops become tackier, and faint are the fragrances of the flower shops, bistros, fruit-and-vegetable stands, and the like. The shops are more overtly commercial, catering to tourists more than to the local people.

One of Paris's great vistas is experienced from Pont des Arts—a delicate iron pedestrian crossing linking the St. Germain district with the Louvre. Nearly an hour before dusk, following a gloriously sunny day, we meandered toward the Seine, along somnolent streets, past shops that would remain quiet perhaps only until the next Monday morning, or until September when most Parisians would return from their summer vacations. From the Institut de France on the Left Bank, we were drawn to this famous crossing where people and musicians gather and stroll, bidding Paris goodnight in the setting sun, which descended behind the Eiffel Tower to the west, as the moon rose above the Hôtel de Ville to the east.

The view from Pont des Arts offers one of the most spectacular perspectives of Paris. One evening a full moon rose beyond the cubic masses that surround the spires of Notre Dame, all glowing orange and yellow from absorbing the remaining moments of the sun. As the full moon rose and cast a soothing spell upon the city, the sun continued to fall and turn the western sky an array of colors, until finally all merged to create a

The Louvre from St. Germain area

soft gradation of purple hues that served as a backdrop to the city, softening its hard urban edges.

When darkness arrived and all color was gone, the city lights of yellow and white flickered, seeming to signify the beginning of another kind of moment in Paris—one that contrasted with the serenity of Pont des Arts at sunset but suggested a multitude of possibilities. It was at this moment that the hypnotic force from the interaction of the city, river, and the setting sun gave way, and those who remained on the bridge moved on and the music faded into darkness.

# The Louvre and the Champs Elysées

*P*erhaps Paris's most popular walk is from the Louvre to the Arc de Triomphe, along the Avenue des Champs Elysées. Contrary to the monumentality expressed by its exterior, inside the Louvre is a conundrum of galleries organized in a fashion not unlike a suburban shopping mall. But the art in the Louvre is magnificent and abundant; if one spent just thirty seconds looking at each work, it would take four and one-half months to see everything. Aside from the art, the new Louvre Pyramid by I. M. Pei has become a major attraction. Visiting the Louvre shortly after the pyramid opened in 1989, I found it a striking success, both functionally and aesthetically. Its pure form and monumental scale seemed in perfect keeping with the grand order of traditional French architecture and planning, brought into the twentieth century through its simplicity and modern materials. On my return visit, however, I found it uninspiring and not nearly so pure or powerful, but rather arbitrary and capricious. Architecture should not be so devoid of unique character that it can be stamped all over the world regardless of site specificity. Each problem should be evaluated so that innovative solutions result not only

Le Louvre

from preconceived notions but from a unique set of parameters.

This is what I believe disturbs the Parisians so much — Pei's defiance of the already powerful historical-physical context. The purpose of the sixty-foot-high pyramid is unclear, and perhaps a less bold approach would have been more appropriate. One of the main requirements of the design was to create a single entrance to the underground so that visitors could easily enter and exit the museum, but the pyramid exceeds its functional demands with little aesthetic gain. A pyramidal form may have been fine in another context, or in a less architecturally defined physical environment, but the vastness of the Cour Napoléon and the richness of the existing, surrounding architecture diminish the urban power of the glass pyramid. Ironically, it needs to be larger to achieve its intended power, but anything larger would have been functionally absurd. This pyramid perhaps is an example of locking into an idea before truly understanding its limitations and consequences.

In spite of the pyramid's weakness in terms of its urban setting, it is aesthetically and functionally successful inside. Seeing the golden stone of the Louvre through the skeletal space frame and clear glass is a wonderful juxtaposition, if only the greenhouse effect could have been resolved. If one were not already uncomfortably warm upon entering, one certainly would be after descending the spiral staircase. Once within the large lobby area the space is vast and simple, but this is fine, as it helps direct visitors to their destinations. The only detail inside the pyramid is the elegant and sophisticated space frame, but there is little else that distinguishes this building from other Pei buildings.

It is difficult to determine if the Parisians' distaste for the pyramid stems from the fact that a Chinese-born, American architect was chosen by Mitterrand over many equally qualified, distinguished French architects, but nevertheless, the building is open to controversy. Only time will tell whether the criticism of the pyramid is rooted in careful thought or is only a temperamental reaction. After all, they despised the Eiffel Tower when it was completed (one hundred years before the pyramid), and today it is one of the most beloved structures in Paris.

Farther west, on axis with the Louvre, stands the Arc de Triomphe

Hercules - Le Louvre

du Carrousel—a miniature arch built by Napoléon Bonaparte to celebrate France's many military victories. Originally, the Tuileries Palace and the *arc* were connected to the Louvre, enclosing the western end of the courtyard, but the palace has long since been destroyed. The result is a free-floating, scaleless object isolated within a windblown wasteland. It does continue the axis, however, which extends to the obelisk at Place de la Concorde, the Arc de Triomphe, and the new Grande Arche at La Défense (the modern business district northwest of Paris).

The axial walk just northwest of the small arch, through the Jardin des Tuileries from the Louvre to the Place de la Concorde, is agonizingly long with little to experience along the sand-laden paths, other than the monuments glimpsed in the distance. Only the occasional tree groves and sculpture gardens provide a slightly more human-scale diversion from this otherwise vast promenade.

While the Tuileries made me imagine the medieval streets that once must have occupied the now painfully formal plot, Place de la Concorde, immediately northwest of the gardens, offered a counterpoint. Its evocative power stems not simply from the square's historic significance, but from its openness to the urban landscape beyond. The bloody events that flooded the square during the Reign of Terror are now mostly forgotten, and the executions committed under the influence of paranoia are remembered with shame and disgust. Place de la Concorde is no longer an inward-focused square, but one that radiates out toward the vast city of Paris. The only hazards to life and health are automobiles, raced flippantly through the square at outrageous speeds.

The breathtaking vistas from the Place de la Concorde offer relief from the endless axial procession of the Tuileries and the Champs Elysées. Endangering our lives, we crossed traffic to the center where the great obelisk of Luxor soars between flanking fountains to the north and south. Though in shade, the gold dome of the Invalides to the southwest shimmered and gleamed as if illuminated from within. The Tour Eiffel beyond contrasted this glow with its punctured flowing lines silhouetted against a clear blue sky. The roofs of the Grand Palais and Petit Palais, rising above enormous trees, hinted at their grandeur and elegance. The Arc de

Triomphe loomed farther to the northwest through a gray haze of exhaust. Directly north the templelike Madeleine, framed by two Neoclassical *hôtels* on Rue de Rivoli and its southern twin, the Palais Bourbon, appeared to be the same size, though in actuality they differ greatly. Looking east, we saw the western entrance of the Tuileries Gardens, flanked by two more Neoclassical museum buildings—the Jeu de Paume and the Orangerie. Perhaps nowhere in the world can one simultaneously view such an array of magnificent monuments, built by men in their continual quest to dominate nature. As the innumerable cars raced by, it seemed from this place that perhaps the men had triumphed.

Facing each other across the Avenue Winston Churchill, on axis with the Invalides across Pont Alexandre III, are the Petit Palais and Grand Palais. Both were built for the 1900 World Exhibition. While both buildings took advantage of the spanning capability of steel, they were designed very flamboyantly and eclectically, reflective of Neobaroque, Rococo, and Art Nouveau styles. Mannerist sculptures, reminiscent of the swirling figures of a Tiepolo painting, animate the roofline of the Grand Palais, particularly at the entrance and end pavilions. Their dynamism adds a vitality to the elegantly ordered and colonnaded facades. Critics have scoffed at these buildings for not being more innovative and embracing the new technology of steel, but their whimsical nature and powerful presence have endured. As more mundane towers of steel and glass rise within La Défense, the Petit Palais and Grand Palais have come to be appreciated.

Continuing northwest on the grand boulevard, one comes to the Rond Point des Champs Elysées, an area that once must have been a fantastic meeting place at the midpoint of the avenue. Today, though a welcome interruption from the avenue's continuous linear progression, it is hardly more than a major intersection where vehicles converge before dispersing throughout the city. If one pauses for a moment at this crossing of the avenue of haute couture, a magnificent view of the splendor of Place de la Concorde can be seen.

Just off the Avenue des Champs Elysées are Avenue George V and Avenue Montaigne. Each is an extension of the fashionable wealth that is

Petit Palais

exhibited on the Champs Elysées, but they are generally much less crowded with people. Lining the streets, strings of Mercedes, Jaguars, and taxis park momentarily, while patrons frequent their favorite stores for a quick fix. It is not uncommon to see couples materially pampering one another, dressed in Paris's finest and most posh fashions.

On Avenue Montaigne, near the famous Plaza Athénée hotel and the clothing store Nina Ricci, stands the Théâtre des Champs Elysées, designed by the architect Auguste Perret in 1909 and finished in 1913. It is a powerful work of almost stark simplicity, but gilded ornaments selectively located enliven the otherwise harsh, rational building. Near the top of the building is a beautiful carved frieze of abstract angular forms, which appears to have influenced the later Palais de Chaillot near the Eiffel Tower, designed for the 1937 Exhibition.

Northwest, on Avenue des Champs Elysées, just beyond the Rond Point and the green of the bordering parks, flashes of neon dominate the street life, and the crowds become more dense. Cafés of enormous scale line the sidewalks—here, their wealthy patrons laugh and sip drinks with an air of dignity while others try to conceal their disbelief as they order the obligatory seven-dollar beer. These cafés are interspersed among clothing shops, movie theaters, airline company offices, and numerous banks, all of appropriate grandness. Though the sidewalks are at least six meters wide, it is impossible to walk swiftly through the leisurely meandering, densely packed crowds; sometimes one must even come to a complete stop. Some buildings are painstakingly decorative, while others bear no ornament at all, but all rise to a uniform height of approximately eight stories and define the edges of this vast avenue. Though automobiles now use this thoroughfare as a freeway to the city, and symbols of commercialism dominate the streetscape, the romance of this avenue's rich past lives on.

Throughout the day the Champs Elysées is mobbed with people who window-shop, sit at cafés, or simply stroll. As I watched on an early afternoon in autumn, most people walked on the northern side of the street to capture the warmth from the sun. In the few open areas between the masses, leaves were scattered and windblown, having fallen from the lush,

Restaurant Laurent, Place Marigny

deciduous trees, which allow one to breathe in the city. The people, automobiles, and leaves were full of color, in contrast with the staid gray and cream-colored stone facades all rising to the same height. At the top are the penthouses, once the living quarters for servants, which now have become sanctuaries for the wealthy to escape from—and overlook—the city. An array of dormers and other windows give character to roofs, while other buildings are surmounted by gardens and simple terraces, sometimes with the exquisiteness of a city park. It was not difficult to imagine the pleasure of being on a rooftop terrace, far enough away from the street to experience serenity, but not so far as to be completely isolated. The views from the rooftops must encompass the immediate neighborhood much more personally than the views one might experience from a high-rise apartment tower in an American city, where one is so removed from the street that sensing the surrounding neighborhood would be unlikely.

Though obviously popular with tourists, Avenue des Champs Elysées is a desirable address for entrepreneurs and businesses as well. Numerous companies vie for a location there, and from building to building, one finds some of the most powerful and wealthy companies in the world—Mercedes, Peugeot, Virgin Records, numerous banks, airlines, various department stores, and restaurants among them. Like New York's Fifth Avenue, Champs Elysées has nothing modest or humble. In mid-September, huge posters of Bruce Willis, armed with his trusty machine gun, adorned the walls of one of the countless movie theaters and greatly contrasted with the more provocative posters for movies such as *Boyz N the Hood*.

It was difficult to determine which stores to enter, but I did wander through the Mercedes showroom. I nearly stumbled over the glued, but peeling, sheet-vinyl flooring, which was intended to look like stone and on which a new convertible, priced at nearly one hundred thousand dollars, was parked. I wondered if the obvious paradox was intentional as a form of subliminal advertisement, but surely most people's eyes were fixed on the shiny, slick automobiles, not the floor, as they tripped into the showroom.

Like that of many of the monuments and squares of Paris, the

Arc de Triomphe

meaning of the Arc de Triomphe has changed over time. Though it still may be a symbol of Napoléon's victories to some, to others it simply represents the grand entrance to Paris. Since it was erected in 1836, some thirty years after its design by Chalgrin, it has played a significant role in a number of ways. The procession of Victor Hugo's funeral began under the arch. The Nazis marched through it during World War II, but shortly thereafter, General Charles de Gaulle led a jubilant crowd through, toward Notre Dame, in recognition of the surrendering Germans. The arch also marks the termination of the famous Tour de France bicycle race. But while the Arc de Triomphe conveys different meanings to each visitor, it always exudes sustenance and power.

From the top, where one is exposed to the winds and open sky, all of Paris appears before the viewer's eyes. A muffled roar rises from the constant flow of traffic around the rotary below, as cars narrowly escape collision in their efforts to enter or leave the city. The paving pattern reflects the twelve streets that intersect at the Charles de Gaulle Etoile, as well as all the identical triangular buildings that rest between the merging avenues. Except for Avenue Foch, which extends west to the Bois de Boulogne, all of the avenues are typically full of cars, buses, and trucks, spewing exhaust fumes that surprisingly have not killed the row of trees that embraces and encircles the arch. Trees extend down many of the avenues, but are most prominent on the Avenue des Champs Elysées, which unabashedly bisects the city from northwest to southeast, through the Tuileries and the Louvre.

Le Louvre

# St. Honoré

The area bordered by Boulevard Haussmann to the north and west and Rue St. Honoré to the south, which parallels the Avenue des Champs Elysées, is commonly referred to as St. Honoré. This area traditionally has been defined as Paris's commercial district, but its character ranges greatly from the Place de la Madeleine to the Palais Royal. St. Honoré perhaps lacks the cohesiveness of other more tightly knit areas in Paris, but it is colorfully enriched by specific isolated monuments, elegant apartment buildings, and generous urban squares interspersed among a plethora of enticing shops.

One of the older—and once one of the most grand—squares in Paris is Place des Victoires. Today, it is not usually among the priorities on the tourist list, but this is unfortunate. The scale and character of Place des Victoires, designed by Jules Hardouin-Mansart in 1685, are much more intimate than the more grand nineteenth-century squares later implemented by Haussmann under Napoléon III. It is enclosed by buildings that relate in scale and materials while maintaining their own identity. Like many other squares in Paris, a central sculpture—in this case a bronze equestrian statue of Louis XIV—serves as a symbol as well as a focus for the many streets that radiate from the square into the city. Unfortunately, this statue is inaccessible, because of the cars that are continually racing around the small rotary in search of one of the six intersecting streets. But fortunately, the perimeter walks adjacent to the shops are the subject of most people's interest. These high-fashion galleries will most probably ensure that this once-noble square will not again fall into ruin as it did in the nineteenth century.

From Place des Victoires, it is a short walk to the Palais Royal, down Rue des Petits Champs, which provides splendid axial vistas north to the Bourse du Commerce and east to Place des Victoires. North of the Palais Royal, perimeter shops and housing provide transition between the city beyond and royal garden within. On our way into the garden, past the elegant restaurants that spill out from the continuous colonnades, the utter silence brilliantly contrasts with the ceaseless city noises of automobiles, buses, and motorcycles. Like everyone who enters the royal garden, we stopped at the peaceful domain encircling the central fountain and basin. Approaching the fountain, we saw and felt the

La Danse, by Carpeaux, at L'Opéra

faint mist that rode the late summer winds, blowing softly in the early evening before the calm of nightfall. People often gather around the water at this time to savor the remaining moments of the sun in peace before moving on to other activities.

Other fountains in Paris may be more beautiful, but few have as tranquil an effect as the modulating fountain in the garden of the Palais Royal. Unlike other Parisian fountains, one can hear this fountain and feel its sporadic droplets sprayed by the light, swirling winds. The garden itself induces tranquillity; it reinforces the notions of repose and order in each aspect of its design. The lime trees are trimmed identically, providing a soft buffer between the garden center and the outer buildings. The continuous repetitive arcade provides another transitional layer between the garden and the perimeter shops. The building's elegant, simple facades are composed of a light-cream stone, detailed with restraint. All reinforce the peaceful separation from the surrounding noisy streets. Aside from the forecourt in the south, with its odd black-and-white striated and truncated columns, the garden at the Palais Royal is not in the least whimsical. But when in the garden, a paradoxical sensation takes hold; while a strong feeling of freedom pervades its quietude and openness, one also experiences a simultaneous perception of security. Whether intended or not, the result is a rare and remarkable balance.

It is strange to think that the character of the palace and garden was not always this way. The three main wings that surround the garden were commissioned in 1780 as a speculative development by the duke of Orléans, who was short on money at the time. The lower level was devoted to shops, cafés, and restaurants, while the upper levels were designated as apartments. Up until shortly after the Revolution, this area was the busiest cultural and commercial center in the city. However, for much of the nineteenth century, it went into severe decline and became the locale of numerous brothels. Today its seedy and vibrant past has vanished, and the area has been transformed from palace, to funfair, to tranquil public garden.

It is hard to argue that the architecture adds to the serenity of the place considering its animated past; Paris of the eighteenth and nineteenth centuries did not need to escape from the noise and pollution of an automobile society. But today everything about the Jardin du Palais Royal is in contrast with the bustle of the surrounding urban environment. The building complex and garden have become, seemingly by accident, what they are best suited to be—an escape from the city within the city. The simple landscaping of two double rows of trees with a central fountain, in conjunction with the restrained, simple (for its own time) architecture that

6 rue Feuillade

surrounds it, is a valuable example of how to achieve beauty through simplicity and discipline.

The area just north of the Palais Royal is in stunning contrast with the garden within the palace. The streets are narrow, noise abounds, and the architecture is richly varied. Still, there are wonderful places of respite within this active area. Two galleries are nestled just east of the Bibliothèque Nationale. One, owned and renovated by the library, is called Galerie Colbert, while the other, Galerie Vivienne, runs parallel to Colbert. These exquisite covered passages lack the neon signs that pervade the galleries I had previously visited. Stores and cafés line the walls and spill out onto the multicolored mosaic floors, blending harmoniously with one another. At its northern end, a minor passageway crosses the Galerie Colbert, creating an exquisite intersection. In the center of the inlaid-stone floor stands a bronze figure mounted on a stone pedestal, reinforcing the circular geometry of the volume, and illuminated by a large, domed skylight. The incessantly changing play of the shadows from the mullions of the dome upon the cream-colored walls, accented by the warm-orange, *faux*-marble columns, was remarkable to watch as I attempted to paint this space in the early evening light. Very few people visited the galleries at this time, making each person's voice and footsteps echo as they passed through this elegant promenade and crossing. Some stopped to look at the shop windows and marvel at the splendid space, while others were more practical and used the gallery as a shortcut to their next destination. Regardless of their many purposes, the galleries of Paris are marvelous urban spaces that would benefit any large city that is prone to extreme temperature changes.

The nearby Bibliothèque Nationale, on Rue Vivienne, is a remarkable complex of buildings built over many centuries. The fortresslike exterior perhaps symbolizes the protection of the extraordinary nine-million-volume treasure housed within. The interior can be just as intimidating; but when visiting it, one must experience the brilliant, grand Reading Room (Salle des Imprimés) by the architect Henri Labrouste, completed in 1868. One of Paris's finest institutional public spaces, this room ingeniously reconciles the tradition of institutional Classical architecture with what was, in the nineteenth century, the emerging technology of iron.

It also provides the grandeur required of a national library while maintaining an intimacy called for by studious endeavors. As in many great libraries, the walls are composed of shelved books, but in the Bibliothèque Nationale, the walls of books also symbolically support the vaults that carry the perimeter domes of the nine-domed ceiling. The detail is rich but subtle, only evident when the treatment of surfaces and structure is carefully viewed. The family of colors and materials works in unison to create a harmonious interior of repose,

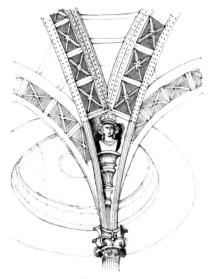

Bibliothèque Nationale

dignity, and strength and also suggests movement, venture, and lightness—opposites that result in balance. This balance is perhaps a characteristic that many learned people strive for.

The Salle des Imprimés at the Bibliothèque Nationale is a further exploration of Labrouste's ideas realized at the Bibliothèque Ste. Geneviève, but this later reading room is considered his greatest work. It is in stark contrast with the opulent Opéra by Garnier, which was built at nearly the same time. While Garnier rejected the use of iron in his design because of its innate inability to respond to proportion and scale, Labrouste embraced it wholeheartedly. By using iron columns as the primary structural elements to support the domed roof, Labrouste avoided massive interior walls, which would have destroyed the open and light effect he desired. Labrouste played off the emphasis on construction ironically to create what must have seemed an architecture that was structurally impossible. The beauty of the Salle des Imprimés lies in its tectonic nature, its celebration of structure and construction to achieve a lightness and delicacy, while the beauty of the Opéra by Garnier lies in its understanding of proportions and scale, all contributing to its solidity and strength. Both are brilliant works of architecture, but whereas the Opéra seems to represent the Second Empire of Napoléon III, the Bibliothèque Nationale is perhaps a critique of this era.

A German scholar, Christian Beutler, has referred to the Reading Room as being the "greenhouse of science, with scholars as its gardeners." This notion stems from the idea that the slender iron columns and the circular domed skylights allude to trees. But while there may be evidence that Labrouste was enamored with a garden at the Luxembourg Gardens where he read in silence under the large canopy of trees, I think the columns and domes are more important functionally than they are symbolically. They address the needs of a reading room for natural light and openness. This garden concept could be further argued in that the lunettes along the east and west walls are painted with bucolic scenes showing trees and blue skies, but Labrouste claimed that these landscape paintings were chosen merely because they would be less distracting to the readers.

While it is unfortunate that electric lights have somewhat negated one of the primary concepts of the Bibliothèque Nationale, it still is a powerful work of architecture that sought the new without dismissing the old. Perhaps more important, its architecture reflects its function — it responds to what a reading room naturally wants to be. While this notion may perhaps seem commonplace, it is a notion that was not too often explored until the period of Modernism, when one of the major tenets of art was to merge both form and function.

Farther north of the Galeries Colbert and Vivienne, beyond the Bourse des Valeurs (Stock Exchange) is the Passage des Panoramas. The elegant purity of this charming passage — approximately twenty feet wide and twenty-five feet high with a skylight at the apex — is undermined by neon signs cantilevered from the walls. It reminded me of Tokyo's shopping streets, where neon is a primary element integrated with the architecture, but in this gallery the neon is simply applied. Nevertheless, the Passage des Panoramas is a peaceful and welcome diversion from the grand boulevards.

Following the Passage des Panoramas to the north is the Passage Jouffroy, decorated by neon as well, but tamed by its stone walls, mosaic

Galerie Colbert

Magazin au Printemps

floors, and especially by the Hôtel Chopin at the northern terminus. The hotel, with its wooden windows and its nineteenth-century lobby and waiting room with fine decor and leather sofas, is reminiscent of that Paris of the past often sought when one strolls through the city's streets.

After a short walk through yet another passage to the north, I came upon Rue du Faubourg Montmartre, which marks the introduction to northern Paris. The abundant restaurant seating that extends beyond the sidewalks onto the street was filled by robust women who sat hunched over in metal chairs, ceaselessly bantering. Down the street men were gathered around a mobile gambling wagon, arguing with the local bookie over cheap prizes from their winnings. The seediness was accentuated further by the decrepit buildings and littered streets. Though separated by only four blocks, neither the ostentatious pomposity of the department stores on Boulevard Haussmann nor the humbly modest simplicity of Rue du Faubourg Montmartre had any effect on the other.

Near the Rue du Faubourg Montmartre is the Place de la Bourse at the Bourse des Valeurs. Built during the reign of Napoléon Bonaparte, the enormous building appears classically poised on the outside, while the Parisian brokers work themselves into delirium within. When I arrived, at dusk, the market had already been closed for a few hours, as evidenced by groups of men in loosened ties relaxing at a nearby brasserie, where they sipped wine in a moment of relative stillness. As the sun was setting, the golden Bourse was illuminated with orange and yellow light, evoking a richness not unlike the splendor at dawn, when the employees would return to their temple.

The streets that intersect and run parallel to Rue St. Honoré are multifarious, causing me to wander aimlessly before eventually ending up at Boulevard Haussmann, where I was awakened from my dreaminess at the department store Au Printemps. This wonderfully whimsical Baroque-inspired building houses numerous exclusive shops. The off-white walls enriched with ornament, fanciful fenestrations with green iron rails and balustrades, and domed copper roofs topped with the ubiquitous elongated Parisian cupolas are a feast for the eyes, and a perfectly appropriate image for a shopping center. Colorful people came and went with exquisite bags stuffed with new clothing and perfumes, providing yet another level of adornment at the street level that added to the already festive character.

In contrast with Au Printemps's refined exterior design, the Galeries Lafayette focuses inward on the lavish, stained-glass ceiling of its domed atrium space. While most visitors were trying to decide between Chanel No. 5 and Byzance, I snaked my way to the atrium to view the grand stained-glass dome. It is like a magnificent piece of jewelry, more beautiful than the numerous gold chains and emerald-clad rings displayed beneath it, yet the dome often goes unnoticed, even though its presence is almost central to the Galeries Lafayette. The atrium is exceptionally inspirational, with its multicolored-glass dome filtering light down four stories, past the convex balconies that project between the stone columns, reminiscent of private boxes in luxurious old theaters. It is the symbol of Galeries Lafayette. If it were eliminated, there would be no focus to the design, nor would there be anything to distinguish Lafayette from any other department store. The elaborate and festive architecture captures the spirit of Galeries Lafayette and is a major factor in attracting people.

After the overwhelmingly exuberant atmosphere of Galeries Lafayette and Au Printemps I walked south to the short, but noted, Boulevard des Italiens. Like Boulevard Haussmann, it was once a great pedestrian-oriented boulevard full of shops, boutiques, and cafés where people came to watch and meet one another. But today, though elegant shops and grandiose apartments still line this street, the automobile rules. The loud noises and the fumes from various vehicles make it a very uncomfortable place to stroll. Symbolic of this transformation is the ever-present McDonald's at the intersection of Boulevard Haussmann with Boulevard des Italiens.

Nearby and contrasting with the disturbing Boulevard Haussmann is the Chapelle Expiatoire, where Marie Antoinette and Louis XVI were interred. It was designed in 1815 on the cemetery grounds where thousands of victims of the Revolution were buried, yet today it stands as a memorial to French royalists. Like many monuments, its meaning has faded with time and finally has become lost. Attentions are now focused on the peaceful surrounding park, which is more popular for its picnics than its historical significance.

At the western border of Boulevard Haussmann is the mid-nineteenth-century church of St. Augustin, by the architect Victor Baltard. It is significant for its early implementation of cast iron, though this was not used as extensively here as it was in the now-demolished Halles Centrales, also by Baltard. St. Augustin appears to be a composite structure, making it difficult to determine where the cast iron is actually structural and where it is simply ornamental. Nevertheless, this use of iron, a modern material at the time, complicates the building's categorization. Its architectural style is very eclectic, neither Baroque, Classical, nor Gothic, but all three. Given these transitional characteristics, it is not difficult to understand why the building lacks a specific identity, but ironically this weakness is also St. Augustin's strength. If it had been constructed completely in stone, it might be just another revivalist church.

At the heart of the commercial area is Garnier's celebratory opera house, which epitomizes the optimism characteristic of the Second Empire under Napoléon III. The exterior of the building is not only a feast for the eyes in all its sculptural appliqué and sumptuous detail, but is also a fantastic example of a clear parti, or architectural concept, with exquisite proportions. It is difficult to forget the essence of the facade, which is all of white stone punctuated with deep, dark openings—arched at the first level and rectangular above. The clarity of the exterior facade reflects a similarly simple parti of the interior, which is detailed even more elaborately with rich materials of various hues. Yet the polychromy and lavish decoration do not overpower the generous volume of the lobby, with its grand flowing stair sweeping gracefully and symmetrically both right and left. The performance hall is splendid as well, and surprisingly intimate considering the capacious volume of the entire building; at the time of its construction, it was the largest and most prestigious opera house in the world. Today, it still hosts musical and other performances, but a new opera house has recently been constructed at Place de la Bastille.

When Garnier was chosen to be the architect after an intensive

*L'Opéra (interior)*

competition, many were outraged, including Empress Eugénie, who asked Garnier why the building had no definitive style. Garnier responded, "Madame, it is Napoléon III, and you complain." This apparently appeased her, but this idea did not please the emperor, who visited the building only once, in 1862, to lay the foundation stone.

L'Opéra (interior)

L'Opéra

Some forty years after the reign of Napoléon III, Le Corbusier, the prolific twentieth-century modern architect, continued to ridicule the Opéra. In fact, Le Corbusier detested the building. Yet in spite of tremendous derision, the Opéra stands as one of the most important works of nineteenth-century architecture and today is not nearly so controversial.

When looking at and experiencing the Opéra, one should keep in mind what the architect intended. As D. V. Zanten observed in *Designing Paris*, Garnier traveled to Greece and perceived for the first time what he thought was the true quality of Classical architecture. He saw emotion and human life latent in architecture. This idea influenced Garnier's thinking about the Opéra, which he saw as the embodiment of man's most primitive instinct: that of gathering together in ceremony around the campfire to share thoughts and dreams, to hear and to see and be seen.

The Opéra is just that. It is a disciplined work, but one of fervent imagination. So just as Labrouste understood the nature of a reading room at the Bibliothèque Nationale, Garnier understood the all-encompassing meaning of an opera house, where life is reflected through intense passion and drama.

Sketching the interior lobby of the old Opéra was, as I expected, very challenging, constantly requiring decisions regarding what to emphasize. If one were to draw all the details ornamenting the surfaces, the drawing would become blackened, and all would be lost. Though it has been done numerous times in hope of better understanding the building, I joined the ranks of those who never tire of this celebrated edifice, which remains a lavish expression of optimism.

I also painted the exterior, amid the suffocating onslaught of traffic encircling the noble edifice and poisoning it with blackened air. I finished the painting, giving the facade colors that really are not there but seem to seep through the walls, erasing the soot and reviving its skin. The Opéra evokes powerful energy as well as calm, hope, and frivolity, despite its location at the center of a vehicular raceway that feeds the grand avenues and boulevards that, ironically, were implemented by Haussmann to purify the city, rather than sicken it.

The original Harry's Bar, where Ernest Hemingway, James Joyce, George Gershwin, and other famous expatriates spent their limited income on tap beer and hot dogs, is oddly situated in St. Honoré, adding another anomaly to this schizophrenic area. Today, Harry's appears to be only a nostalgic remembrance with few customers; it no longer exudes the mystique it must have once possessed. American college pennants still hang from the walls, and bartenders still serve draft beer and hot dogs, but the majority of visitors are curious tourists who read the old newspaper clippings on the walls and search for their alma mater's pennant.

Just a few blocks away is another famous square called Place Vendôme. Jules Hardouin-Mansart, architect to Louis XIV, designed the formal facades that surround the grand square, which originally had yet another equestrian statue of Louis XIV at its center. As a result of the Revolution, the statue was demolished, and what we see today is a 132-foot-high bronze monument modeled after Trajan's Column in Rome. In 1871 this column was the object of political and aesthetic vandalism, masterminded by the revolutionary painter Gustave Courbet. When the Third Republic took power, Courbet was ordered to restore the monument, but he fled to Switzerland to avoid doing so. Nonetheless the column stands today with Napoléon dressed as Julius Caesar mounted atop it. During the Revolution, Place Vendôme was known as Place des Piques as a result of nine anti-revolutionary victims' heads being displayed on spikes, but today all that is on display are Rolex watches, massive diamonds, and various under-designed, overly extravagant jewelry. Only time will tell how history will change the meaning of Place Vendôme.

La Madeleine, another mammoth temple constructed under the rule of Napoléon Bonaparte, has a commanding and overwhelming presence. The Corinthian columns, each one at least twelve feet in diameter, dwarf the individual who stands atop the monumental steps within the portico. This stark, blackened, windowless building, originally designed as a temple of glory in honor of the Grand Army, contrasts with the perpetual motion and lavishness that surround it. The vehicular road encircling La Madeleine is reminiscent of Grand Prix raceways, yet one tends to forget the traffic when distracted by the exquisite shop windows. Of particular interest is Fauchon, where every day various foods are meticulously arranged with such artistry that one doesn't want to touch the food for fear of disturbing the beautiful still life. The atmosphere is almost sacred. I noticed a few minutes after entering Fauchon that I had removed my hat—a custom I typically reserve for visiting churches. Perhaps this is not surprising, as this temple of beautiful food displays untouchable vegetables and forbidden fruit with a similar demand for reverence.

Our long and varied walk through St. Honoré ended at St. Roch. Like St. Germain des Prés, St. Roch has been marked by violence in Paris's

St. Roch

history. The bullet holes still visible in the front facade were the result of a harsh skirmish between the royal troops and home forces in 1795. Ten days after the outburst, Napoléon Bonaparte, a twenty-seven-year-old soldier involved in the fight, was named commander in chief of the home forces. The church was closed, but we managed to find a vacant step at a shop on Rue St. Roch, from which we admired the sinuous yet bold edifice. We sketched quickly as the sun faded and washed the front facade, creating long, curved shadows, sweeping along the convex and concave surfaces. Again, it was hard to believe that violence could have occurred in a place characterized by such beauty.

# The Marais

The Marais (once marshland, hence its name) is nestled between the Bastille to the east and the Pompidou Center to the west. It is one of Paris's oldest and most intimate areas, and the one least affected by the city's accumulating wealth. Our stroll there ironically began at the uncharacteristically grand and barren Place de la Bastille. The glitzy and enormous new Opéra de la Bastille confronts the windy square like a modern-day fortress, but nonetheless provides a focus for this vast and disorienting area. It was designed by Carlos Ott of *NORR* in Toronto in 1988 as a result of an international competition sponsored by the French government. It has been said that Mitterrand mistakenly chose Ott's design thinking it was the work of the American architect Richard Meier. While much larger in terms of seating capacity and more practical than Garnier's opera house, it is not nearly as dramatic or monumental. From afar, this building expresses fluidity as well as power, both entirely appropriate for its location and function, while appearing as a unified and permanent part of the urban fabric. Yet when one walks closer to the structure, it is immediately apparent that in concept the forms presided over the materials,

Opéra Bastille

as evidenced by the already chipped and cracked veneer of stone and pre-cast concrete that reveal its hollow construction behind.

To the west of the new opera house are the dark brown cobble-stones that outline the now-destroyed walls of the old Bastille, where the Revolution began more than two hundred years ago. The Bastille, built in 1370, had originally served as a palace for nearly two hundred and fifty years, but at the time of the Revolution it was being used as a prison — with temporary holding cells reserved for the elite of Parisian society — because it had become outmoded as a palace. One of the most noted pris-oners held there was the famous "unknown prisoner," masked in black vel-vet and thought by some to have been Molière.

At the time of the onslaught by the revolutionaries in 1789, the prison was already in a sad state of decline, perhaps terminally ill. Though few people died in the siege, and only nine prisoners were actually re-leased, the storming of the Bastille sparked a fervor that changed France forever. Over time, following the Revolution, the area surrounding the Bas-tille fell into a state of decline, but it is hoped that the new opera house

St. Marie de la Visitation

will add needed energy to this recently directionless and uneventful square, which symbolically marks the eastern entrance to the Marais and Paris.

After a *café* in the hot sun at a corner brasserie, and a sketch of the church of Ste. Marie de la Visitation, by François Mansart, we proceeded north to the Hôtel de Sully, built from 1624 to 1634 by Jean Androuet du Cerceau. It still stands proudly despite years of decay. Though originally designed for a notorious gambler (professionally a banker), who lost his entire fortune shortly after moving in, the *hôtel* is most remembered as the seventeenth-century residence of the duke of Sully, a minister to Henri IV who lived there with his much younger wife. She was well known for the affairs she readily carried on, and which the duke supposedly hardly minded; he apparently even had a private stair installed for convenience' sake. This private mansion, once the most elaborate of its kind, is now primarily an information center. But its character still evokes the spirit of what was once the most fashionable and intellectual area in Paris. Before and during the seventeenth century—the heyday of the Marais—seven kings resided in this district, including Henri II. His mansion occupied a site near the Place des Vosges, but shortly after its completion, his wife, Catherine de Médicis, ordered the demolition of the mansion in an attempt to erase the tragic memory of her husband's untimely death.

One can enter the Place des Vosges through the southwest corner of the Hôtel de Sully. One afternoon a pair of young female violinists played under the arcade in this discreet corner. Such elegance seemed entirely appropriate; the music made it easier to imagine the many aristocrats who had resided there in the seventeenth century. In Place des Vosges an air of dignity emanates from the graceful town houses that surround the perfectly proportioned square, which was probably designed by Clément Métezeau between 1605 and 1612. Both grandness and intimacy are sensed at Place des Vosges; one feels neither diminished nor claustrophobic. Though the town houses are nearly identical in design, with a balance of brick and stone resting above a continuous ground-level arcade, the environment is not at all static. The various shops, ever-changing shadows, flickering sunlight, the trees, grass, sculptures, and most important the people add dynamism and color to this pedestrian-oriented square.

Place des Vosges

When first completed, Place des Vosges was one of only a few open areas that contrasted with the narrow huddled streets of Paris. Though there are many open squares in Paris today, Place des Vosges remains unique in that its character has changed very little, except for the constant flow of residents. Madame de Sévigné no longer peeps from her window to record the follies of the aristocrats, but others may now gaze from the same window, perhaps absorbing the present-day tranquillity and the subtle interludes of human experience.

The beauty of Place des Vosges prompted me to return many times. Its walls, columns, pilasters, windows, door knockers, and other elements show their age but live on under the care of proud tenants. Some columns seem to struggle not to sink into the earth, but the essence of the buildings remains unchanged. The steeply pitched slate roofs reveal various light and dark stains, resulting not only from the intensity of the sun's rays, but also in response to natural aging. Chimneys penetrate these roofs at the east and west wings at heights equivalent to the apex of the roofs on the King's Pavilion and Queen's Pavilion. While the external world is faintly visible through these pavilions' grand archways, inside one smells the hint of dying leaves rather than automobile exhaust. And the pleasant sound of the spraying fountains is altered only by nature's breezes, rather than the sounds of traffic. The square is not a passageway to hasten one's travels, but rather to absorb life's subtleties.

In the center of Place des Vosges is the grinning statue of Louis XIII, beneath the natural canopy of a circular double row of trees. He seems to watch all that transpires from there, facing the south wall with its deep-red brick that has faded to terra-cotta on the north wall from the intense southern light. On this wall the Queen's Gate and Pavilion briefly interrupt the stone arcade visible beyond the trunks of the carefully manicured trees and the cast-iron fence that encircle and define the square. Gas lamps and ever-flowing fountains mark the four corners of green where people read in the sun, away from the more frequented benches under the central umbrella of leaves that fall to the paved earth. Such is the setting of Place des Vosges, which graces the area of the Marais. It is a haven not to be missed.

Leaving Place des Vosges, passing through the King's Gate and Pavilion—a four-story pavilion that stands high above the surrounding five-story structures—one comes to the Rue de Birague, which resonates with the character of the Marais. The buildings lining this street are various and serve the locals of the neighborhood. A laundromat stands adjacent to a small hotel; an Italian bistro neighbors a clothing store. The workers at the clothing store eat lunch at the bistro, and the restaurant employees probably respond in kind by buying their clothes there.

Another street just north of Place des Vosges—the Rue des Francs Bourgeois—bisects the Marais. This Jewish section of Paris, which begins at Place des Vosges, runs parallel with the Seine until it reaches the Archives Nationales at Rue des Archives. Elegant clothing shops with newly painted wood storefronts, bright new canopies, and clean windows are scattered along this richly textured street, but for every new shop there are older counterpoints. Despite the occasional flashes of neon, most of the signs are simple and are fixed to the surface of walls above the storefronts. Additionally, many of the corner buildings still have old carved-stone street signs. But it is good to see the newer painted signs, appearing above them, reveal the same names, which often recall significant French people who once resided in the Marais. Above the street level, ornamental wrought-iron rails signal the more recent buildings, while most of the older buildings are ornamented by wooden shutters only. Some are crooked and stained from years of wear; others are straight and newly painted but in complete keeping with their original character. Periodically, a rush of cool air blows through the exhaust grilles built into the bases of new storefronts, but in spite of this intrusion by modern technology, the Marais is a long way from being transformed into yet another fashionable street mall.

Rue des Francs Bourgeois is heavily traveled by motorcycles, automobiles, and delivery trucks, but the noise does not seem to deter pedestrians. It is a street characterized by an architectural vitality that has resulted from years of transformation. Its vernacular quality is something an architect could never imagine or create, yet we are drawn to such streets by this quality. There is no such thing as a typical street block in this area; one block may be eighty feet long and interrupted by intermittent alleys, while another may be a continuous one thousand feet.

The fabric of this area is composed of four- to six-story stucco-faced apartments with simple, utilitarian doorways and windows. These simple houses, of various natural hues of brown and gray, reveal their age and structure through cracks in their weathered skin. Additionally, they lack the celebrated ornament of Paris's many *hôtels* or its nineteenth-century apartment buildings dispersed throughout the city. Mansard and gabled roofs, with a variable rhythm of small dormers, neighbor flat, terraced roof-scapes, creating a syncopated skyline. This disparate array of roofs, separated by tilted stone chimneys penetrated by numerous orange-tiled flues, appears stacked like a house of cards ready to fall. All of this makes for a marvelously rich composition as well as a remarkable example of urban individualization, nonetheless achieving a cohesive composition.

Though some walls along the base of Rue des Francs Bourgeois have been cleaned, one can still see the remnants of graffiti. Other walls, set ten to fifteen feet back from the street, thus protected from vandalism, are nonetheless blackened with soot and pigeon excrement near the base. But all are light and clean near the top, washed by the sun and removed from the filth of the exhaust. The sun also washes the stone-laid sidewalks on even the narrowest streets. The walkways are made of two sizes of cobblestone — eighteen-by-twenty-four-inch stone pavers compose most of the walks, interrupted by six-by-six-inch cobblestones, which are found only at entrances and drives. The smooth stones, infilled with concrete mortar joints that vary in width, are a variety of yellows, oranges, and browns, but their colors have been subdued with gray from years of wear. In contrast with the richly textured walks, the asphalt-paved street slopes toward the curb in irregular swales from years of settling. As a result of being built on marshland, the buildings also have settled in awkward ways, especially the seventeenth-century *hôtels*, which span hundreds of feet. Lintels droop and sills bend at small angles in relation to the walks, but perhaps the settling was abrupt and the walls will remain as they are.

As noted, this lively street is also graced with elaborate grand-scale *hôtels* with rusticated stone bases and enormous stone archways, interspersed among the more common stucco dwellings. The archways mark entrances to the seventeenth-century *hôtel* courtyards, which originally provided a buffer from the activity of the streets, as well as a place for a carriage to enter from the street. These courtyards further served as organizers to the symmetrical **U**-shaped plans of the mansions. Today, some of the courts are primarily paved with cobblestones, while others have been transformed into gardens filled with flowers, trees, and shrubs, with simpler utilitarian drives, but in all cases they still provide a clear transition from the public to the private.

In the northern section of the Marais, just east of Rue Vieille du Temple, is the Musée Picasso, housed in the seventeenth-century Hôtel Salé. It is the largest collection of Picasso's works in the world, and though it has only a few "masterpieces," it presents a chronological display spanning Picasso's life from adolescence to death. In the first room are a number of

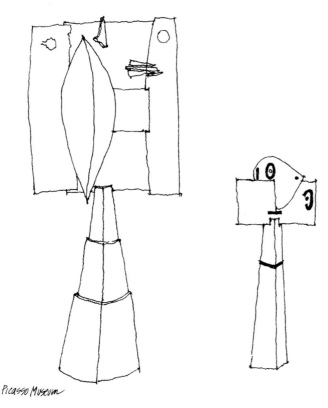

Picasso Museum

Picasso's Tête de Femme, Picasso Museum

portraits done by Picasso when he was between the ages of fourteen and twenty. All of these paintings demonstrate his understanding of composition, color, and the human figure. They represent Picasso's traditional training in the discipline of painting. Picasso's experimentation with Cubism began only after he had gained an understanding of the more traditional forms of representation and had mastered the medium. One can see in his later Cubist works an influence from his earlier paintings of the French countryside and farm buildings; it is not difficult to see how Cubism evolved from the essence of these earlier paintings.

Progressing through the museum, one senses the extraordinary variety and proliferation of Picasso's explorations. Some works are extremely simple and two-dimensional, with only intense primary colors, while others are full of texture and depth with a full range of color. With few deviations, the subjects of Picasso's paintings are people or the human figure—he never stopped searching for new expressions of life. His work explores the ranges of human emotion, from ecstasy to intense sorrow. When one leaves the court and enters the streets of the Marais, the area does not appear as it was before—things are seen differently. It is appropriate that in a city where one can find "everything," there is a museum that also demonstrates enormous range and the vast expressions of art—those of a single human being.

After being simultaneously numbed and awakened by the Musée Picasso we found our way to the nearby Hôtel Lamoignon, where the writers Flaubert, Turgenev, and Zola frequently conversed with Daudet when he resided there in the late nineteenth century. This *hôtel* is across the street from a small restaurant where we had enjoyed a splendid brunch on our last trip. As in New York, weekend brunch in Paris is an afternoon affair—an almost-religious event. On Sundays, the dank streets of the Marais are typically quiet; most of the shops are closed; automobiles hardly seem apparent; but hints of life are seen beyond the doors and windows of the various restaurants as employees prepare exquisite meals and patrons spoil themselves with conversation and food. One can enjoy tranquillity without going to either a park or the countryside and can feast on some of Paris's richer morning fare.

In the spirit of things, I too partook of brunch one Sunday at the oddest of places—odd in a lovely and wonderful sense. On Rue du Temple, at the intersection with Rue des Blancs Manteaux, a courtyard that may once have been part of an *hôtel* today is the focus of the Marais School of Dance. On the south end of the court, a Mexican restaurant serves a very popular brunch, while people enjoy the continuous beat of music and watch the dancers practicing various repertoires beyond the windows of the many halls that surround the court. Near the entrance to the court, to the north of the archway, tap dancers feverishly rehearsed in front of a large mirror. In the adjacent north wing, couples seductively tangoed in between greeting visiting friends. Through the school's large French windows, which punctuate its painted-stucco facade, above the archway, dancers became animated with quick and impulsive movements in response to the percussion instruments. After nearly an hour they opened the windows and rested their feet on the iron balustrades. Also on the second floor of the south wing, ballet dancers artfully balanced control and movement until the heat of the sun, which beat through the large windows, became too intense, forcing them to change clothing in an attempt to stay cool.

Upon leaving, I looked back on this court and saw the rear wall settling differentially (perhaps the result of the vigorous tap dancers). The lintels were sloped to one side, sills were cracked, walls blackened, and the roof undulated as if it would cave in. But the enthusiasm and energy of the artists overcame these archaic conditions—it appeared dance transcended all else.

Rue des Rosiers is a short street that lazily cuts its way through the heart of the Jewish area in the Marais, from Hôtel Lamoignon in the east to Rue Vieille du Temple in the west. Late on a sunny Tuesday afternoon, I was greeted by a few vagabonds, seated on the sidewalk near the Hôtel Lamoignon, who quietly harassed all passersby for a few francs. Half the shops on the street were open, but beyond the doors of those that were closed one could hear the sounds of saws and other mechanized tools. The diverse variety of shops—a clothing store neighboring a kosher pizza restaurant, across the street from a cutlery—was unified by the insignia of the Star of David.

The street was not crowded, and most who passed through were alone, young and old alike. Children were dressed in traditional attire with yarmulkes, while the older Jewish men, with long dark beards, wore black suits and homburgs. Automobiles rarely passed through this street, so almost every sound was distinguishable. An older man whistled on the narrow southern sidewalk, while a crazed delinquent, with a long scraggly black beard and a slight limp, staggered through the middle of the street shouting obscenities to all who crossed his path. Most ignored him, but when he incited any response, he would burst into laughter and raise his bottle of wine above his head. Still, most people went on unfazed; thus I was assured that he was a local who was familiar and probably harmless.

In the late afternoon on Rue des Rosiers and the nearby Rue des Francs Bourgeois, young women shopped for dinner, carrying their baguettes and sacks, sometimes on foot and other times on bicycles. Many men visited their favorite cafés and stood to drink beer and smoke a few cigarettes at the bars before going home. The cafés in the Marais are small and unpretentious; they are places where friends meet and briefly socialize, unlike the posh and expansive cafés near Les Halles and the Pompidou Center where people sit for hours observing, smoking, drinking, and reveling in being watched.

An old barbershop near the end of Rue des Rosiers at Rue Vieille du Temple was open as well. Its wooden storefront, which sloped to one side, was painted blue, and in the windows were photos of movie stars from the sixties and seventies. In the dark space beyond, an elderly man, who must have been nearly eighty years old, hunched over from years of work, was cutting a young boy's hair. I watched momentarily before turning off this old street that tenuously clings to its past as the surrounding streets try to move into the future. I wondered how many more children would have their hair cut at this old shop. Will someone else replace the old barber when he leaves his legacy?

At one moment all appears crumbling and decrepit in the Marais, but without warning an old *hôtel* may appear, restored to the beauty and grandeur of its original presence, but heightened amid the fabric of simple stucco buildings. But the charm of this area is not just its grand *hôtels*; it is the joy of constant discovery. The Marais does not have a Notre Dame or Panthéon; it has only the woven conundrum of streets that breathe differently than the rest of the center of Paris, which has remained unscathed by Haussmann's grand plans. It is interesting to note that these labyrinthine streets, once passages of squalor and filth, now inspire nostalgia and romance. And Haussmann's panacea — the grand boulevards — choke under the filth of carbon monoxide and smother the unlucky facades with a black film that only neon can overcome. At the westernmost reaches of the Marais, at Boulevard de Sébastopol, a plenitude of neon calls all consumers to partake of its excess. It is here, bordering the modern warehouse of art (Pompidou Center), that one is readily shocked and awakened from the wistful nostalgia induced by the medieval Marais.

■   ■   ■

Rue des Barres

When Paris was being redesigned according to Haussmann's scheme of grand monumentality and formal axiality, Père Lachaise cemetery, northeast of Place de la Bastille, was designed as a romantic interlude. Ironically, over the years the cemetery has become a healing ground for those who seek momentary peace and a rest from the crowds in the city center. It is a place where many privately pay homage and silently speak to the many artists who have been buried there. Many literary figures who were first buried elsewhere were later moved to Père Lachaise. As I wandered up the hill toward the east on narrow tree-covered pathways, I came upon sarcophagi erected in the memory of such notables as Molière, Balzac, Haussmann, Abélard and Héloïse, David, Seurat, and others.

Most of their tombs are in great contrast with the more traditional Gothic-inspired shrines, which had small enclosed spaces where visitors could pray and leave offerings of flowers. Apollinaire's tomb is engraved with poetry about his tortured and misunderstood heart; Oscar Wilde's has a sculpture of a winged man aiming north, barely floating above the surface of the simple white-stone base; Proust's is a simple, black, reflective-marble tomb unadorned except for a sculpted cross. All were laden with flowers from those who still remember and ardently follow. Wilde's grave even had notes from visitors, which rested upon a ledge, thanking him for shedding light upon their lives. Far to the east in the cemetery lies Gertrude Stein, still treated as a pariah even after death, isolated to the most distant point from the entrance. Her tomb faces the nearby factory buildings, and unlike most of the other shrines it is exposed to the sun, unprotected by trees.

After discovering many of these important shrines, I moved on past the more common Gothic structures, obelisks, and even grand tombs reminiscent of *chedis* in Thailand. Eventually I came upon the largest structure in the cemetery—a Byzantine-inspired building with striated stone and a large flat dome with two towers rising beyond it. A freestanding two-tiered arcade, with numerous colorful tiles mounted on its walls, surrounded the structure on all sides. I encircled the temple and coming around the back saw a small, unornamented opening at its base, which opened onto the driveway that passed through a wrought-iron gate. First I thought the opening must be where a casket would be brought in, but

Tomb by Viollet-le-Duc @ Père Lachaise

after noticing smoke rising from what originally appeared to be minarets, and having heard the flames churn from within, I realized that this was the crematorium.

Many people were picnicking that day on the scattered benches dispersed throughout the cemetery. Some seats were filled by elderly people who appeared to be regulars; they probably tarry there daily, picking up after visitors as if tidying their own backyards. Other seats were filled by teenagers in search of Jim Morrison, dead or alive. Taking a seat on one of the benches, I wondered at the contrast between the fastidiousness that Paris shows for its dead and the careless neglect by which cities fall into ruin. Père Lachaise is a work of art that will probably remain standing long after our cities and will serve as an important testament for future generations. But today it would be hard to design a tomb for a cemetery in the United States; the prospect would seem absurd to most. We live in a society of "now" and the future; memories, recollections, and respect for the past are most rare. Père Lachaise and other places like it are rare indeed; they must be preserved, at least as symbols of what once was.

# Les Halles

ordering the Marais to the west is the area remembered as "the belly of Paris" (as Emile Zola put it), where twelve grand iron-and-glass canopies once covered a central marketplace. Unfortunately, this market—Les Halles Centrales—was destroyed in 1971, but shortly thereafter the nearby Centre Georges Pompidou, otherwise known as Beaubourg, and the Forum des Halles were constructed, and life was restored to this once-lively area, which had regrettably begun to decay. Only the Bourse du Commerce and St. Eustache and simple residences scattered about this area remind us of what was.

The outrageous Beaubourg, an anomaly in Paris that itself seems to be performing for the city, is further animated by a plethora of street performers and "artists." However, loiterers and drunks add a lewdness to this area that is sometimes disturbing, but most often this is somehow dulled by the Pompidou Center's vitality and magnetism, which are exceeded by few places in the world. It is a stage for the bizarre and provides a haven for the disavowed, but in all its grotesqueness it attracts more people than any other place in Paris. One wonders if it would be nearly as

*Bourse du Commerce*

successful if it were located elsewhere. By its extraordinary contrast with its context, it is apparent that there is nothing else quite like the Pompidou Center. It stands alone amid the dense urban mass of load-bearing walls and steep-pitched slate roofs, and unlike its neighbors, it hides nothing and revels in exposing its innards in a variety of hues that accentuate its abnormality.

The Centre Georges Pompidou was designed by the Anglo-Italian team of Richard Rogers and Renzo Piano, who were selected from a field of nearly seven hundred in an international competition. It has been argued that the museum, finished in 1977, was built as an attempt by then-president Pompidou to reassert France's cultural and technical superiority. Whether it does this is a matter of debate, for in all its technological wizardry it also exposes to the outdoors all that normally needs to be protected (structural and mechanical systems). The structural system articulately expressed and the mechanical systems colorfully identified are what distinguish the Pompidou Center, but this is not entirely done for stylistic purposes; it also allows maximum flexibility of the interior. Interestingly,

Pompidou center

this concept was also utilized by Henri Labrouste in his library designs of the mid-nineteenth century, but at the Pompidou Center it has been pushed to its limit. The space is nearly entirely open and flexible, and the highly articulated technology serves as a new kind of ornament. Circulation, spatial organization, structure, mechanical systems, and ornamentation all work harmoniously together at the Pompidou.

Fast-food restaurants, such as Free Time and Pizza Hut, mark the gastronomically abundant entrance to Place Georges Pompidou from the north. Across from these restaurants a few loiterers typically lean on the concrete bollards that define the edge of the square. Nearby, a wall cuts diagonally through the square, dividing a segment of the plaza between it and Rue Rambuteau, which is the only constantly vacant area of the square.

Typically, an array of performers and onlookers fill the other portion of the large square, which inclines down toward the building. On one Monday afternoon, just south of the diagonal wall, Peruvian musicians played simple instruments as they danced and intertwined among themselves in a circular motion. Many onlookers tapped their feet in subtle celebratory approval. Meanwhile in the center of the plaza, an Asian woman was picking up her assortment of rags and heading elsewhere for lunch. This diminutive woman often dances there in agonizingly slow motion, seemingly moving in a trance to hypnotic new-age electronic music, draped in torn cotton coats that flow with each movement. Her motions, though incredibly controlled, are what one might imagine a baby's would be like while still in its mother's womb. She seems oblivious to the surface of the plaza, which is often covered with paper cups and broken glass that eventually flow naturally to the base of the slope. She attracts significant numbers of people who watch with varied expressions, most staying for quite a long time, as if equally entranced by the dance and music.

At the southwest corner of Place Georges Pompidou, a group of harmless older vagrants resides on the sloped cobblestone paving; they appear as permanent fixtures of the setting. Nearby, at the corner of Rue St. Martin and Rue St. Merri, a group of men is always huddled around a single orator, perched atop a milk crate, who speaks swiftly and apparently with cunning wit to an audience that will debate with him about most anything.

If stumped by his interrogators' questions, he must concede his reign and someone new takes the pedestal.

The various artists who perform within the open forum of Place Georges Pompidou are the constants of this area of inexhaustible variety. In the context of the Pompidou Center, with its insides unnaturally exposed, any of these unique events appears quite natural. Nothing would seem strange there, except for normalcy.

In the early evening, the colors of the Pompidou Center appear saturated, while the adjacent church of St. Merri glows as if from a powerful hidden light source. The smell of filth and the sounds of breaking bottles are ever present at the Pompidou, and they grow more fierce as darkness swallows the square. The mood and focus change greatly as well, as the street performers count their daily take, and the recently full square suddenly empties, appearing vast and nearly desolate. The magnetism that inundates the area during the day is no longer evident. The only life that remains is the vagrants on the southwest corner and the group of men still huddled around their master of ceremonies, engaged in apparent heated and angry debate constantly broken by bursts of laughter. As the evening progresses, even these groups vacate, and the square becomes entirely vacant except for the cans, beer bottles, and trash scattered about the stone paving, reminiscent of a littered public beach after a hot summer day. But on returning to this square in the morning, one would find the trash cleared away by green-clad, government-employed street cleaners. Every morning they can be seen at work throughout the city.

Adjacent to the Pompidou Center is Paris's most colorful and humorous fountain, *Le Sacre du Printemps*, in Place Igor Stravinsky. It is perfectly appropriate that Stravinsky, a proponent of dissonant music, should have an honorary square in Paris's most cacophonous district. Colorful and vibrant kinetic-sculpture fountains, reminiscent of Picasso's figures of the 1920s, dance atop a basin of water spraying mist in all directions, to most everyone's amusement.

One evening, at the whimsical fountain, I decided to do a simple sketch of Beaubourg from the continuous, smooth aluminum bench that encircles the fountain. I had already attempted a simple painting from a

Pompidou Center from Place Igor Stravinsky

different location, but soon I discovered that there is no such thing as a simple sketch of Beaubourg. The technologically inspired building makes any impressionistic sketch more insulting than complimentary. Drafting the Pompidou Center in straight, clean lines would be more appropriate. The result of my sketch was rather crude, but it did interestingly suggest the building's rapidly decaying nature. As I continued drawing, the colorful array of fountains in the foreground faded into indistinguishable silhouettes with the dimming light of evening. Beaubourg grew quiet, its colors reduced in intensity. Only the enormous white structure reflected the last semblance of the sun's light.

The previous descriptions of the Pompidou Center and its immediate surroundings contradict the usually romantic notions often held about Paris. But adjacent to the infestation of neon-lit shops and various fast-food joints are some extremely popular first-rate cafés designed by France's most progressive contemporary architects. Elegantly dressed people sit outside at the tables that overflow onto Rue Berger, ironically facing the Fontaine des Innocents, where nomads and backpackers sing and laugh, living in a world unknown to most. Café Costès, recently designed by Philippe Starck, is one such café. It is enormous, with a grand, elegantly designed central stair that leads up to a mezzanine and down to space-age bathrooms in the basement. The bathrooms are quite elegant, but the untraditional fixtures leave one confused; these bathrooms should not be frequented by those more accustomed to straightforward toilet arrangements.

■　　■　　■

Bourse du Commerce

In shocking contrast is the section of Rue St. Denis just to the north of the Pompidou Center. Once a great entrance road to the city, this street has been transformed into the heart of Paris's red-light district. Smoke-filled, greasy restaurants, brightly lit sex shops, and decaying apartments line and define the street, while countless scantily clad prostitutes stand in unlit doorways, only their bare legs reflecting the neon lights. Though promiscuity has never been kept secret in Paris, it has become limited to fewer areas of the city. However, on Rue St. Denis the smells of urine and perfume, and the signs of the business, are powerful. In the evening the path generally has one purpose, but during the day men, women, and children walk up and down the street seemingly unfazed by the posters and flashing signs above the windows, and doors with drawn beaded curtains. One almost expects to see Henry Miller emerge from behind one of the doors or drawn curtains, but it seems that no one ever does. Closer to the new Forum des Halles, the sex shops become more scarce, but they still infiltrate the area, only eventually to become subsumed amid other theatrical phenomena.

Northwest of Place Georges Pompidou, foreign to the world of Rue St. Denis, is a quaint pedestrian street called Rue de la Petite Truanderie, filled with numerous cafés, restaurants, and wine bars that are scattered about under large trees. Only the colors of the tablecloths distinguish one restaurant from the next. During lunch one afternoon a crazed man wandered from restaurant to restaurant performing in hope of making some money. At one restaurant, he bellowed as if he were Luciano Pavarotti, and at the next he performed in a deep tortured voice, claiming to be Salvador Dalí. People grinned and chuckled. Hardly annoyed, some even gave him a few francs.

Emile Zola once wrote that the cast-iron structure of Les Halles Centrales would set the tone of architecture to come, and it did. But ironically, while Les Halles are no longer extant, the neighboring stone cathedral of St. Eustache still remains. Although St. Eustache is graceful, it appears incomplete. Built from 1532 to 1640, it was designed as a Gothic structure, but with a Classical architectural vocabulary. St. Eustache was intended to rival

Café L'Esplanade near St. Eustache

St. Eustache

Paris's most grand cathedrals, and though it failed for many reasons, it remains one of Paris's most important churches. In the nineteenth and early twentieth centuries, workers might have frequented this church before shopping at the nearby Halles Centrales, but today, St. Eustache stands proudly facing the paved open court to the south, where curved stone seats and mounds of grass create an informal public amphitheater. The continuous sounds of the fountain fill the air and drown out the sounds of the automobiles, sometimes aided by musicians who help to soften the harsh city noises.

The Renaissance-inspired western facade of St. Eustache does not conform at all with its predominantly Gothic structure; it faces the Rue du Jour, which is lined with cafés that are often filled with young students enjoying beer. This facade of St. Eustache is sadly inconsequential because it doesn't have a grand square facing it like the southern facade, and most people don't experience it from the west, but it is beautiful, nevertheless. At sunset, it can be luminous, as if glowing from within the golden stone wall itself.

Farther north on Rue du Jour, following the contour of the church of St. Eustache, the character of the street transforms from the vast openness to the south. Few cars navigate the narrow street. The older secular buildings that remain appear to cascade from the church in deference to the flying buttresses beyond; they appear to cling to the church's walls, tainting its apparent purity. But St. Eustache also clings to the few surrounding crooked buildings, suggesting an affection for the area's deep-rooted past prior to the vast demolition of 1971.

When evening arrives at St. Eustache, crowds still surround the church to the south, some in meditative silence, others absorbed in wine and dance. It remains a stage open to the sky, secure from the seductive lure of the glitzy Forum des Halles.

# Montmartre

The Montmartre area possesses an urban richness and diversity unique to Paris. The streets wind and climb the hills, which offer wonderful vistas over the city below. After an enjoyable walk through the streets of Montmartre, it also became clear that few prominent buildings exist there; it is more of a functioning urban village. But on Avenue Junot is a house designed in 1926 by a famous pioneer of modern architecture, Adolf Loos of Vienna. This house for Dada artist Tristan Tzara is Loos's only work in Paris, but it exhibits much of what he wrote about and practiced. Though the house responds to the artist's disposition toward art by, in some ways, rejecting anything historical, it also is a further development of the *raumplan*, or "plan of volumes," that Loos developed in Vienna. The *raumplan* explores architecture through a very complex interior spatial organization in which there are many levels distinguishing particular functions. In some ways this idea emanates from the organization of medieval architecture, but whereas medieval architecture most often resulted in a picturesque exterior ensemble, Loos's buildings defy this by being very staid and symmetrical. Loos never seemed to free himself from

Montmarte, view toward Sacré Coeur

this rather formal exterior expression, and the Tzara house is no exception.
Its exterior is stripped of any ornament and is completely symmetrical.
While the lower level is composed of rough stone, and the upper levels of
smooth stucco, there is little suggestion of the complexity of the interior

Perhaps only coincidentally, the exterior neither contradicts nor respects the surrounding urban character, except by its mere height. But this simple expression seems perfectly appropriate for Montmartre—an area that is beautiful precisely for its lack of pretension. Loos despised architecture that pretended to be something it wasn't. He felt everyone wanted to make themselves out to be something more than they were. Loos desired an architecture that represented the values of modern man, not one that was built on historical styles out of fear. While Loos may not have truly exercised his ideas, they contributed significantly to the development of other Modernists such as Le Corbusier, who was better able to realize Loos's treatises.

In the northern section of Montmartre, on the back side of the hill, we briefly ventured down Rue du Poteau, sometimes referred to as one of Paris's prettiest street markets, before beginning the slow ascent on Rue du Mont Cenis toward the monumental Sacré Coeur. Rue du Mont Cenis is a vehicular road until it intersects Rue Francoeur, where it changes into a series of stairs offering magnificent views down Rue du Mont Cenis and north of the city. On a clear day one can easily see the cathedral in the town of St. Denis seven miles north. The residences that ascend this street simply follow its natural contours, gracefully stepping up the hill. Once it reaches a higher plateau, a residence may be only two or three stories high, but from its lowest point on the street it may be as many as eight stories.

As we walked east on Rue Cortot, the major dome of Sacré Coeur became visible above the nearby cafés and shops. Its stillness and power amid the madness of consumerism are inspiring. At the base of Sacré Coeur various street musicians try to earn a living by their art, whether it be tap dancing, 1920s-style jazz, or African percussion instruments, which inspire the passersby to move to the rhythmic beat.

After encircling Sacré Coeur, we settled in a delightful park called Parc de la Turlure, northeast of the church. We both were inspired to sketch what we thought was the more interesting, less recognized view of the great church. It was nearly sunset when we finished sketching, and again we circled Sacré Coeur to join the masses in the front. Pink and gray clouds rolled above the domes, their various hues echoed in the marvelous

Sacré Coeur

white stone of the church, now draped in soft shadows. But the serenity of the moment became more faint as we meandered farther down Paris's version of the Spanish Steps to the base, where crowds of people and the sounds of automobiles overpowered the great church. Once at the base, looking back at Sacré Coeur rising above the decorative carousel and the street performers, I was reminded of the power of built form, for architecture is a wonderful measure of our values and culture, but more important it is the fruition of our dreams, aspirations, and imaginations taking us beyond the mere reflection of temporal life.

Once removed from Sacré Coeur, I remembered our last visit in the spring of 1989, when very few people had been there. To the left of the front facade an elegantly dressed man had sung opera with great and moving passion, while a gentle elderly man stood at the base of the grand steps to feed a flock of hovering birds; they ate from his hand with a trust that could only have come from many years of ritual and kindness. Considering the immense popularity of Sacré Coeur and its usual inundation with hoards of visitors, I am fortunate to have such a unique memory.

If one visits Montmartre a number of times, its essence and appeal are revealed. In Montmartre one can witness the vicissitudes of the common person's life. The narrow and sloping streets are lined with concrete bollards that protect pedestrians from passing vehicles. The squares are neither grand nor focused on central equestrian statues. They are simple, canopied by trees and bordered by straightforward wooden benches. The buildings are similar in scale to other apartment buildings in Paris, but for the most part lack the eclectic ornament and decoration borrowed from Renaissance Italy. No signs of Haussmann's radical plans of grandeur are apparent in Montmartre; nor are there many cultural monuments that help define or give focus to neighborhoods. But modest churches, which barely rise above the stuccoed walls defining the edges of the streets, are scattered throughout Montmartre. And atop the hill, the ubiquitous soft-white yet bold church of Sacré Coeur pierces the horizon and rises above all to establish the spiritual center of Montmartre.

■　　■　　■

9 Rue Joseph de Maistre, by H. Cambon

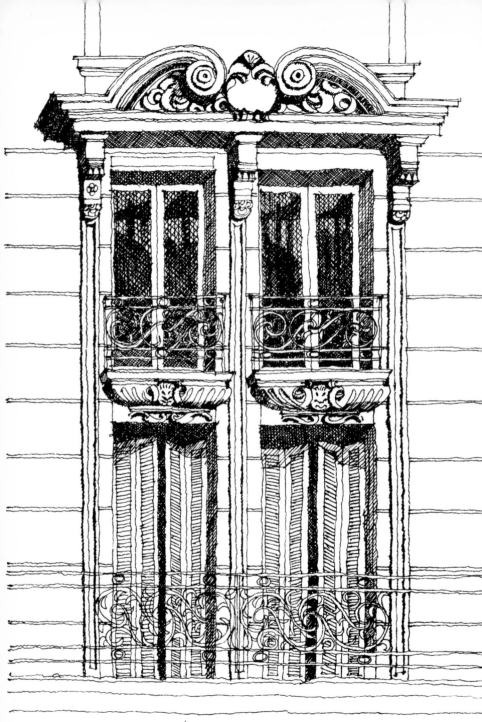

Montmartre, rue Joseph de Maistre

130

While the destitution of fin de siècle Montmartre, as described powerfully by Zola and other writers, is less evident today, an aura of seediness still pervades the southern edges of this area, particularly in the evenings just south of Place des Abesses near Place Blanche and Place Pigalle, which are linked by Boulevard de Clichy. This street thrives on the young and naive in its attempts to perpetuate its decaying existence. The romance and excitement, described by Henry Miller and others compelled by this mournful existence, are lost to most, but still it fascinates, even if only in the stinging splashes of neon that promote sex, toys, and peep shows. The grim delight in chafing at death and bankruptcy is no longer evident as it was during the dark days of absinthe, rampant prostitution, and drunkenness; but Montmartre still clings with integrity to its forthright lack of pretense. It consciously tries to distinguish itself from the charmed and fashionable streets of Paris.

As for the artists who now reside and display their work at Place du Terte, they hardly compare with the great masters of the late nineteenth and early twentieth centuries, but many do appear to make a fair living. One day, while I was painting at the corner of Rue Norvins and Rue St. Rustique near Sacré Coeur, a man drove up in a Mercedes-Benz and parked nearby. He opened the trunk of his car and pulled out numerous canvases painted with scenes of Paris. His work was hardly innovative, though it was quite competent, and while he surely should not be scorned for making money as an artist, I couldn't help thinking of struggling artists such as Vincent van Gogh, who knew almost no monetary success. If it were not for such artists who had helped in creating the almost mythical aura of Montmartre, the artists who paint there today would hardly be recognized, but for a few exceptions. Place du Terte is full of talented, technically skilled portraitists, but if one is searching for passion or greater insights into the world of art, there may be better places. Still it is an exciting place to visit, full of energy and vigor for life.

Though simple and inelegant, the environs of Montmartre are perhaps more authentically Parisian than the rest of "old" Paris, which borrowed heavily from Italian styles. The architecture of Montmartre exists not to impress, but merely because it responded to what was needed. In

Abesses Metro by Hector Guimard

the words of Emile Zola, the "penumbra of melancholy" is more easily read in Montmartre, where there are no ornamented surfaces to disguise its true self. One could say the buildings are clad in well-fitted jeans and a casual shirt, in contrast with the tuxedo worn by the apartment buildings that typically line the grand boulevards throughout the center of Paris.

Sacré Coeur

# Western Paris

T

he area defined as the Sixteenth
Arrondissement, bordered by the vast Bois de Boulogne to the west and
the Seine River in the east, lacks the cohesive character of many other areas
in Paris, but amid the anonymous mid-rise apartments, it contains a number
of interesting anomalies and landmarks of modern architecture.

The architecture of this area contrasts greatly with the ironically
more common, flamboyant Baroque apartments that were concurrently
built in the early twentieth century. Hector Guimard, the designer of the
Art Nouveau canopies that gracefully mark the entrances to many Paris
Métro stations, also designed a number of buildings in this area. His Ecole
du Sacré Coeur on Avenue de La Frillière is in many ways a precursor to
buildings later implemented by Le Corbusier and his followers. This former school is a multistory building in which the more solid upper floors
are raised above a predominantly glass enclosure at ground level, thus giving it the appearance of a structure that floats above the earth's surface.
(Ironically this was inspired by the theoretical principles and revolutionary
forms for iron set forth a half century earlier by Viollet-le-Duc, an im-

portant nineteenth-century architect and writer known primarily for his renovation of Notre Dame.) It is a rational building, which elegantly expresses its structure, particularly at the ground level where pairs of painted iron columns, splayed like open scissors, carry the load of the floors above. The building is unusual for Guimard in its lack of organic ornament and undulating walls, which characterize his other, later work.

Guimard's nearby apartment building on Avenue Mozart is perhaps the finest example of his architectural style. This colorful and fluid five-story structure greatly contrasts with the surrounding stone apartment buildings of brown and gray that echo one another's facades. The refined entrance frames exquisitely crafted doors of wrought iron, whose ornamental infill twists and swirls like vines in nature. The rectangular windows around the building are surrounded by various ornately carved stone frames, each of which is unique. The French rails around the building also vary according to their location. Some are simple, with two horizontal rails spanning only one window, while others are much more complex, spanning many windows. This sophisticated artistry and craft transform the entire facade into a work of sculpture.

The foyer is not at all grand, but the floors are elegantly designed in mosaic tiles, again with flowing lines emulating nature. In most of Guimard's apartment buildings, as at Avenue Mozart, the stairs sweep down from the second level, wrapping around a small lift enveloped with ornamental screens. The flowing balustrades and handrails reinforce the almost liquid nature of the building, in which all elements work harmoniously.

122 Avenue Mozart, by Hector Guimard

Castel Béranger, by Hector Guimard

Guimard's buildings are pleasantly playful, particularly in juxtaposition to the static neighboring apartments, which lack individuality and distinctiveness. Though Guimard was awarded a prize by the city of Paris for his Castel Béranger in 1898, the popularity of the Art Nouveau style of architecture was unfortunately short-lived, largely because of its demand for handcraft in construction and its incompatibility with prefabrication. Much of the design of these buildings was determined on-site during construction, under the supervision of the architect. This way of designing was not uncommon until recently, but today's economic and legal demands make it rather impractical. Though in contemporary practice many decisions are still made in the field, it is not ideal and usually results in conflict among all parties. Unfortunately the best design resolutions often do not come about; we frequently value design less than the more pressing demands of time and money. Nonetheless, architects must accept these stringent factors while still trying to instill poetry and individuality into their architectural designs.

As is the case throughout Paris, this area has a generous share of parks. Under a typically blue September sky, Parc Ste. Périne, bordering Avenue de Versailles and paralleling the Seine, was full of children rolling and running through the stunningly green grass. Other children roller-skated and skateboarded with fearless vigor as elderly people passed cautiously en route to their selected benches. Mothers patiently watched from the surrounding green wooden benches bordered by a colorful array of flowers blooming as brightly as on a spring day. Only walking through the park could one smell the fragrances of the yellow roses, gently carried by the cooling breeze from the nearby Seine. Parc Ste. Périne was beautifully manicured, without a spot of trash, full of blooming flowers and lush green vegetation—one would never have thought that autumn had arrived. The setting was reminiscent of an early, warm spring day that evokes energy and optimism. I feared that on my return to the United States, the parks would appear sadly neglected and lacking in grace in comparison.

Nestled among large apartment towers, some of polychromatic brick and tile, others of minimally ornamented stone, is the Fondation Le Corbusier. Originally it was designed as an apartment where Le Corbusier lived in 1933. Intended as a "machine for living," it is still in great contrast with the surrounding towers in its stark simplicity, entirely void of any ornamentation. The building appears misplaced, nestled in the trees, rising low above the street. Its pure white walls and ribbon windows with aluminum frames do indeed give one the impression that it is something like a machine, but inside it is evident that Le Corbusier's artistic intuition presided. The skillful interrelationship and manipulation of volumes, both horizontally and vertically, and their relationships to the outdoors evoke an ambience more akin to that of a personalized museum than a "machine for living." Le Corbusier's spatial sculpture was the basis for much of his modern architecture, which other architects vainly attempted to emulate, but ironically Le Corbusier's imitators achieved exactly what he claimed to be doing—they created machines for living, working, and playing, buildings that lack the quality that Le Corbusier's house so clearly embodies.

The spirit of Le Corbusier's house is highly idealistic; nothing is present to recall the past, and it evokes a black-and-white mentality with little room for personalization. It is so restrictive in its attention to volume as well as in its utilitarian nature that its character is more aesthetically powerful than most traditional apartment buildings of the same period. Paradoxically, in its attempt to respond to the needs of the "modern man," it dictates what those needs may be. Le Corbusier seems to have failed to realize that homes are more than merely utilitarian; they are the places where individuals can freely express themselves in response to their personal identities. To paraphrase philosopher Karsten Harries, the home is the place of physical and spiritual dwelling in the world.

Near the Le Corbusier Foundation are a number of apartment towers by Robert Mallet-Stevens, most built in 1927. His work is also generally "modern," but unlike Le Corbusier he was not enamored of prefabrication; thus, by Modernist standards, his buildings are considered gratuitous. After seeing them I was thankful for this very gratuitousness. Rather than being ordinary, these bland white structures are more reminiscent of factory buildings than residences. Mallet-Stevens's work is limited to this area of the Sixteenth Arrondissement, and after a short-lived but vigorous period of accomplishments in the 1920s, his work never fully developed or grew with the Modernist movement.

While Guimard sought to bring the organic beauty of nature to architecture, and Le Corbusier looked forward to the machine, Auguste Perret tried to strike a balance between new technology and Paris's historical context. At the turn of this century his architecture embraced the new technology of reinforced concrete, yet it did not dominate or control his architectural expression. Perret's buildings are simple and do not employ the Classical vocabulary of their context, yet they imply a logic similar to that of their neighbors. Tall French windows with iron balustrades—sometimes projecting in bays, other times recessed within the walls—create the primary order for his buildings, just as in the more traditional apartments. His buildings are not typically surmounted by mansard roofs with repetitive dormers, but the roofs step in accordance with the surrounding steeply pitched mansard roofs, again keeping in character.

At 25 Rue Franklin is perhaps Perret's most magnificent Parisian apartment building. A revolutionary building from 1903, it takes full advantage of the capabilities of reinforced concrete by employing a maximum area of windows on the exterior as well as having a flexible interior floor plan (reinforced concrete structure offers much greater flexibility than steel, which generally must follow a structural grid). Yet the large area of glass is only a part of what makes the building unique. Perret also introduced color and craft into this building by using prefabricated, mass-produced, and surface-mounted tiles, which surround the window openings. In front of the window openings, prefabricated ornamental rails, though much simpler than the neighboring balconies, maintain a cohesive spirit, while adding another layer of interest to the facade. The building facade undulates with bays that surround a recessed open court facing the street, not only providing a buffer from the street but also offering a variety of views over Paris past the nearby Tour Eiffel. Perret's apartment building has been criticized by architectural purists for not being singular in its concept, yet its eclectic balance is its very strength. It doesn't reject past ideas and forms out of a need to be different, yet it is unique. It embraces technology and the future, yet technology does not dictate its expression. Perret used geometry and volume to create rhythm and hierarchy without relying on ornament and elaborate detail, yet he did not reject ornament; he realized the importance of expressing the element of craft in buildings. Just as humans need to dress themselves differently to express individuality, buildings need to be embellished. Artistry and craft in architecture give subtle personality to the building and memory to the artisans who fashioned it.

Adding to the anomalies of western Paris is the Palais de Chaillot, on Rue Franklin and on axis with the Eiffel Tower, across the Seine. It was designed by Carlu, Boileau, and Azéma for the 1937 World's Fair and is reminiscent of the Fascist architecture of Germany and Italy of the same period. Its massive stone walls are devoid of windows, ornamented only with enormous relief sculptures carved in stone panels every seventy feet and lines by the poet Paul Valéry inscribed in gold letters. But unlike the Panthéon, whose windowless walls were purposely filled in, the walls of the Palais de Chaillot were left barren intentionally. After a nearly endless solid plane with very little relief, a magnificent void opens to the Eiffel Tower across the Seine. The view is splendid and diminishes the overbearing monumentality of the palace. Perhaps its grandness and powerful horizontal sweeping lines are appropriate for such a soaring and prodigious neighbor as the Eiffel Tower.

Near the Tour Eiffel, the *bateaux mouches* embark on a river tour to the islands and back. This worthwhile ride allows a glimpse of much of Paris in a short period of time, without creating a feeling of haste or distraction.

West of the Eiffel Tower, bordering the Bois de Boulogne at the terminus of the Jardin du Ranelagh, is the Musée Marmottan. This museum is a rare gem, where one can view art without the constant disturbances experienced at Paris's major museums. The focus of the collection is Impressionist works, particularly a significant collection of works by Monet, most of whose paintings in the collection were completed while he resided in his country home in nearby Giverny. These works embody great vigor and reveal Monet's extraordinary awareness of all the senses. His canvases bring to life the mood, time, weather, and even smells he sought to capture. Seen together, these paintings create a greater sense of reality than any photograph could capture.

Monet

Nearby, in the Ranelagh Gardens, an old carousel with wooden horses is tended daily by a sturdy older woman with enormously strong forearms. The youngsters who invade the grounds in the early afternoon throughout the warmer months ride unaware of the slow decay of the carousel and its antiquated gadgetry; but as these past treasures remain by the perseverance of the human spirit, the woman will undoubtedly see to it that the carousel continues to run as long as she does.

Across the Seine on the Left Bank of western Paris is the famous Eiffel Tower. Though the area surrounding the grand monument is rather undefined and vast, it is accented with several important and diverse attractions. One is the esplanade that precedes the Hôtel des Invalides, spanning from the flamboyant Pont Alexandre III. Like many other garden parks in Paris, the esplanade is a classically inspired, linear park lined with trees; it terminates at the long facade of the symmetrical Invalides buildings. This group of buildings was built by Libéral Bruant for King Louis XIV in 1676 to house the kings' elderly and crippled soldiers who had been injured in war. Once completed, it housed six thousand men.

Entering the complex, one passes through a garden, surrounded by a low wall and a moat, which serves as both a transition and a border of this complex of buildings. While such a grand processional and transition through many spaces may be a bit excessive for the approach and entry to most buildings, this rudimentary idea generally can be implemented in a variety of ways and at different scales. For example: In a residence it is a richer and more pleasant experience to pass from a covered entry to a vestibule and foyer before entering the formal rooms of the house.

After passing through the ceremonial gate at the Hôtel des Invalides, one enters a different kind of outdoor space paved in cobblestone and defined by punctured stone facades rather than trees. At the southern end of the court, another adorned portal marks the entrance to the Eglise St. Louis des Invalides, a modest church by seventeenth-century standards that was used by the "invalids" who were housed in the quarters surrounding the main court. Today these quarters house an army museum. Beyond the smaller church is the grand Eglise du Dôme, designed by Jules Hardouin-Mansart in a French Neoclassical/Baroque style. It was commissioned by Louis XIV and is another example of architecture intended to be enjoyed by future generations and symbolizing the king's rich and noble past. Ironically, beneath the golden dome erected by the Sun King rests the tomb of Emperor Napoléon Bonaparte, designed by the Italian architect Visconti nearly twenty years after Bonaparte's death. His sarcophagus is surrounded by tombs of his fellow soldiers and brother. Not sharing the surprisingly reverent adoration for this former ruler, I respectfully viewed the interior from the foyer as visitors encircled the sepulcher below, admiring the Egyptian-inspired tomb and paying homage to one of the world's greatest conquerors.

In great contrast with the cold and militaristic stature of the Hôtel des Invalides is its neighbor, the Musée Rodin. Rodin's house and studio from 1907 until his death in 1917 provides a magnificent, tranquil escape from the grand sprawl of the surrounding cityscape. The intimate scale, superimposed on the symmetrical and axial organization of the classically inspired garden in the rear, conveys a pleasant informality. Sculptures of bronze and stone adorn the intersecting walkways, some dappled in flickering light filtered through the trees, others washed entirely in sunlight. In

Les Bourgeois de Calais, by Rodin

the front court are bronze copies of three of Rodin's most famous works —
*The Burghers of Calais (Les Bourgeois de Calais)*, *The Thinker (Le Penseur)*, and *The
Gates of Hell (La Porte de l'Enfer)*. The tortured visages of the burghers are set
under a canopy of trees where the light flickers upon their figures, further
accentuating their powerfully expressed anguish. In the late afternoon, one
can best appreciate the complexity and richness of the horrifying and
beautiful *Gates of Hell*. The wildly and sensually contorted limbs and bodies,
caught as they flood through the gates, express an inexplicable truth that
transcends reality. Inside, the museum exhibits primarily a chronological
display of Rodin's work, but when I visited it was the work of Camille Claudel that moved me most. Though there is only a small area in the museum
that displays Claudel's work, there is a passion in these sculptures that exists only in the best of Rodin's. Her work seems to reflect her own tragic
and tortured life. After a successful apprenticeship and unsuccessful love
relationship with Rodin, Claudel spent nearly the remainder of her life in
an asylum.

■   ■   ■

Monument of Victor Hugo
for Palais Royale, by Rodin

Le Penseur, by Rodin

Tour Eiffel

The soaring Tour Eiffel is visible from numerous areas in Paris, but perhaps nowhere more impressively than from the Champ de Mars to the southeast, where one can proceed toward the tower as if walking down the nave of a great cathedral. With each step the utter simplicity of its monumental expression—seen from afar as a smooth line—focuses into a rich interweave of iron, and the tower's complexity becomes more clear.

With the autumn sunset the Eiffel Tower reveals delicate patterns unseen earlier in the day. Under the high sun the tower appears as a mass, a bold ascending line, interrupted only by the three platforms that mark the base, middle, and top. However, the orange intensity of the western light illuminates the complex intricacy and sophisticated pattern that unite to create the simple but grand expression we all know. The Eiffel Tower is a clear expression of late-nineteenth-century technological achievement, intentionally embellished with iron ornament. If it had not been articulated with this ornamental iron, the design would likely have failed. The intricacies of the ironwork give the Eiffel Tower another subtle layer of character that does not distract from its essence, but rather acknowledges the importance of embellishment and craft; it ingeniously balances the expression of technology with the suggested presence of a human element.

On another late-summer day, I had the pleasure of viewing the tower at the start of sunset from across the Seine at the Palais de Chaillot, where the fountains left a cooling mist in the air nearly two hundred feet away. Attention revolved around the water flowing from the fountain, which contrasted with the massive facades of the Palais de Chaillot beyond, but as the sun faded and created fractured rays of red and yellow, the fountain receded in importance, and the massive Eiffel Tower absorbed the light. Its brown-iron framework became golden and again revealed its delicate intricacies. The view from the elevated terrace at the palace was stirring. The great tower of iron appeared to rest upon a dense, verdant bed of trees and broad extended planes of grass. All that was visible beyond was the ill-planned tower of Montparnasse on the Left Bank. The classically inspired Ecole Militaire terminates the vast horizontal plane of the Champ de Mars and leads one's eye back to the dominant rising frame, which emulates the bold and fine complex textures found in nature.

# La Défense and Parc de la Villette

$\mathcal{T}$he area one mile northwest of the Arc de Triomphe is the business district called La Défense. Most of its buildings are steel-and-glass towers resting atop a vast platform, which is a central square. In one of his numerous attempts toward immortalization, Mitterrand implemented the construction of the most immense and impressive building at La Défense: La Grande Arche. This magnificent structure extends the major axial procession of the Avenue des Champs Elysées farther northwest from its origin at the Arc du Carrousel in the courtyard of the Louvre, and also aligns with the Place de la Bastille farther east. The enormous arch offers the hope of order to an otherwise undefined area to the west, where odd and lonely apartment towers of undefined scale and texture, spotted with repetitive windows, rise above vast green lawns in defiance of human dimension or individuality. This area embodies many of the ideas about cities that Le Corbusier professed in his book *Vers une Architecture* (1923).* While logical, and minimally accommodating the needs of contemporary living, the area lacks the soul, vitality, and com-

*Translated as *Towards a New Architecture*

plexity that a city can only obtain from years of growth and change. It breeds isolationism and alienation. These tall, residential buildings deny any sort of individuality and, more important, destroy any sense of community or neighborhood. The creation of a neighborhood calls for more than undefined open areas and large towers. There needs to be diversity in the architecture, its spaces, and especially in its functions. The areas in the Latin Quarter and St. Germain are successful as neighborhoods because there is diversity, with shops, residences, schools, churches, parks, and other physical environments intertwined to provide richness and a sense of place.

But most who visit La Défense hardly look beyond La Grande Arche—their eyes focus toward Paris in search of the distant but aligned Arc de Triomphe, which appears minuscule in comparison with La Grande Arche. The arch rises slightly above the trees that encircle it and is incessantly shrouded in a purple-gray haze that hovers just above the entire city, pierced only by the slender construction cranes, reminiscent of ships' masts cutting the dense fog.

La Grande Arche, designed by Johann-Otto von Spreckelsen in the early 1980s, follows Paris's tradition of innovative urban monuments. Exiting from the glass-enclosed train station with its grand sweeping arched roof, designed by the architect/engineer P. L. Nervi in 1957, one is immediately struck by the station's relative monumentality. In comparison to the arch it doesn't loom nearly so large. On a sunny day, the presence of the arch, with its white stone cladding, is as blinding as the sun it reflects. From the proximity of the plaza, one can look at it for only a few seconds; from the base of the enormous staircase, the overwhelming reflections from the white Carrara marble seem to envelop the area in a brilliant light. This immaculate staircase lacks both handrails and balustrades, enhancing the pure expression of its pristine templelike quality, transcending utilitarian requirements. Toward the southwest from the top of this stair, an enormous and barren paved square unfolds, void of any trees. It is accented only by an arbitrary diagonal white path and enormous, colorful abstract sculptures, similar to those found in the public squares that front high rises of the 1970s in Chicago or New York. There is no evidence of

La Grande Arche

the automobile, but somehow even this form of life is sorely missed here —
at least it would provide some semblance of human activity. The "modern"
towers at La Défense are not capped by spires or domes like those in the
center of Paris, but by large corporate logos—the lifeless signs of Esso,
GAN, Manhattan, and others only cause further alienation. The setting
would provide a perfect environment for a futuristic film like *Blade Runner*.

East of the square, a row of shooting fountains creates a translucent vertical wall of water that softens the rigidity of the towers behind. Beyond this fountain are rows of wooden benches, reminiscent of church pews, where people quietly sit and photograph the high-rise buildings symbolizing capitalism, which has apparently become a new religion. While La Défense reminds us of our great technological capabilities, it is also evidence of our frightening ability to conquer the natural environment. Ironically, this man-made "environment" fails to accommodate any human intervention. The human need for change and spontaneity requires the vicissitudes of living in a rich and unpredictable environment; to inhabit a place that pretends to be faultless denies both the human dimension and spirit.

While the commercial district of La Défense exudes a modernity reflective of our technological age with an alienating force, the new science-and-technology park called Parc de la Villette in the northeast of Paris looks forward yet retains many notions and ideas that will always be important in the design of the urban environment. These contradictory driving forces undoubtedly result in radically different experiences: La Défense alienates; Parc de la Villette attempts to respond to human scale and the experiences of the pedestrian. Visiting the park two years earlier, I found it to be a whimsical and arbitrary conglomeration of interesting yet unrelated architectural objects. On returning, however, the clear organization and "stylistic" cohesiveness became readily apparent. While much of Parc de la Villette remains unfinished, there is already a wonderful balance of architecture and green space, all woven together by the continuous covered gallery, which acts as an organizing circulation spine. Inspired by the ancient architectural form of the gallery, it is implemented with materials and structure that respond to today's changing and developing technology. In form it is reminiscent of an undulating sine wave. The red follies designed by Bernard Tschumi are elegant jewels that not only adorn and provide a counterpoint for the vast verdant lawns, but also house a variety of services for visitors; for example, one is a café, another a children's day-care center. While similar in their scale, color, material, form, and structure, each folly abstractly evokes a different image appropriate to its function. They also help as landmarks within the vast seventy-five-acre site that once was home to the slaughterhouse district.

In addition to the main gallery, an elevated east–west walkway cuts through the site, which also allows the visitor to be oriented within the vast area, while connecting a number of pavilions carefully situated along the axis. North of the parallel Canal de l'Ourcq is the Géode, an immense, spherical projection hall clad in stainless steel mirrors, which reflect all that surrounds it. Only the already oblique red follies do not appear any more bizarre as they are distorted by the reflection in the mirrored sphere. The purity of the platonic sphere recollects the spirit of monumental conceptual design by the eighteenth-century French architect Etienne-Louis Boullée. While the reflective purity of the sphere is powerful, it does not capture the sublime grandeur and power evident in Boullée's sketches; however, unlike his design—perhaps in keeping with the practicality of our own age—much of the space within is utilized. North of the sphere, a structural-steel cage frames and supports an enormous older building, now the science museum. In its inside-out structural system, this building recalls the spirit of the Pompidou Center, though it is much more controlled and draws much less attention to itself.

Perhaps the most interesting structure at Parc de la Villette is the southernmost building, the Cité de la Musique, by the architect Christian de Portzamparc. This complex of forms and functions is playful and sinuous without appearing irresolute or arbitrary. Like the collection of red follies, the music complex is composed of a series of parts, ingeniously integrated to form a whole. The simply stated southern facade, facing Avenue Jean Jaurès, extends the urban fabric, but within the park the building changes character; it becomes a free-form and inward-looking complex of masses. Through the manipulation of forms, window sizes, variation of height, differentiation of the roof, and so on, this single building appears as a richly varied complex that truly expresses the variety of activities housed within. However, despite the array of geometric forms and modulating scale, a unity results due in large part to the commonality of materials.

Cité de la Musique in Parc de la Villette

Rotonde de la Villette, by Cl. Ledoux

The park is innovative and progressive, but not without logic and a clarity of purpose. In time, when the large structures, small pavilions, and landscaped gardens are complete, and all have matured beyond their present ephemeral newness, it will be interesting to see what becomes of this grand gesture. I believe its deep-rooted logic and clarity will allow it to remain one of the most successful and inviting urban spaces in Paris. In the future, perhaps the now-in-vogue red follies, catenary curves, and cafés will come to be better appreciated, as have other Parisian defiances of tradition that are presently among its most well-known symbols.

But the Parc de la Villette does not isolate itself in its uniqueness. In the tradition of Parisian urban planning, it engages the city and its other monuments through a larger scheme that creates sometimes subtle interconnections. As mentioned, the second elevated walkway extends through the site parallel to the Canal de l'Ourcq, terminating at the piscine (pool). This peaceful canal, bordered and defined by a long, tree-lined prome-

nade, extends from the northeast of Parc de la Villette to the Place de Sta-
lingrad, some two miles to the southwest where it is submerged beneath
the Rotonde de la Villette. This magnificent terminus to the canal, designed in the second half of the eighteenth century by Claude-Nicolas
Ledoux, originally served as a tollgate along the outer wall of Paris where
visitors paid taxes to bring various goods in and out of the city. The classically inspired, golden-stone building greatly contrasts with the theatrical
architecture that flourished throughout Paris during the same period. Its
beauty lies in the material itself, in the simplicity of its forms, and in its
lack of ornament. A two-storied cylinder, punctuated by arched openings,
penetrates a rectangular volume that is square in plan; four one-story, pedimented porticoes project from each of these facades. There is no super-
fluous ornament, only space and mass. While seemingly monumental and
bold in its clarity, it is nonetheless remarkably humble in comparison with
most of the new bicentennial projects previously discussed.

# Chartres

*D*uring an extended visit to Paris, a trip to Chartres cathedral can be very inspirational. The town of Chartres offers a charm and innocence, in spite of the ever-present commercial signs of tourism. The cathedral dominates the town just as it did in medieval times, and though it is not architecturally pure in concept, its spires and walls express a powerful and entrancing wisdom. Inside, the windows incessantly shimmer and change, revealing hidden stories from the Bible. In the low autumn light, when the sun's rays shine more directly on and through the multicolored translucent planes, the effect is especially powerful. Red and green light flickers upon the stone floors and columns, throughout the southern aisle. The points of the meticulously constructed groin vault align precisely despite its age. One cannot help being in awe of Chartres.

The resident historian of Chartres, Malcolm Miller, whisks visitors through the cathedral with his enthusiastic and brilliant historical analysis of some of the windows. He occasionally interrupts the vigorous tour for a moment of respite, but all the while, he cites from memory, with

Chartres

absolute confidence, wit, and wisdom, the vast knowledge the windows at Chartres have to offer.

While today fewer people than in medieval times make the pilgrimage to Chartres to witness the shroud supposedly worn by Mary at the time of her death, people from all walks of life still come to the cathedral. It is rare that one is not spiritually stirred by this exalted church that continues to teach as it has for eight hundred years. Malcolm Miller would certainly attest that this church is the greatest "book" of medieval times, epitomizing the medieval purpose of architecture, which was to educate and guide. The creation of the printing press irreversibly changed the role of architecture—it eliminated the need of teaching within the physical confines of the church; it was even feared that the printing press might destroy architecture. But it lives on, and even occasionally continues to elucidate some aspect of life.

# Epilogue: Au Revoir à Paris

On my last day in Paris I wanted to experience it all over again, but of course this was impossible. I began my day as I often had, with a bowl of fresh yogurt, followed by a croissant from the nearby Moule Gâteau—at the local outdoor street market on Rue de Lévis that I visited daily. Though it was cool and threatening to rain, I didn't want to ride the Métro anywhere. My legs were strong, and I was determined to explore by foot.

I first stopped at the elegant Parc Monceau late in the morning before the rain began. This whimsically playful and picturesque park is just south of the apartment in which we stayed, in the Seventeenth Arrondissement. As usual, runners circled the park on the dirt-paved perimeter path as older people sat on their usual benches along the main east–west axis, observing all that passed, and elegantly dressed businesspeople traversed the park on their way to work. Near the western border, many schoolchildren played with a daunting energy, in contrast with the normal serenity of the environment. The park is full of wonder and complexity for such a small area. There are two axes—one running north and south and

Parc Monceau

Parc Monceau:
Colonnade at Basin

the other east and west—and in between are meandering paths and a number of romantic follies. A miniature pyramid is set amid trees, plaster copies of sculptures from antiquity line the walkways, ancient Roman ruins sit in fields of beautifully tended grass, sandboxes are scattered adjacent to the paths, a carousel spins near the northern entrance, a stone bridge crosses over a stream which leads to a basin surrounded by a colonnade, and nature's delights abound. But most important, the park is always full of people. Its diversity attracts all kinds of individuals: old and young, professionals and nomads.

In addition to the wonders within the park's wrought-iron gates is a prominent eighteenth-century tollgate designed by Ledoux. This powerful piece of architecture at the northern entrance is reminiscent of Bramante's Tempietto in Rome. But rather than being situated in a court like the

Ledoux's Tollgate, Parc Monceau

Tempietto, Ledoux's tollgate stands proudly alone, terminating the axis of the Rue de Phalsbourg to the north. Originally, it was one of a pair of tollgates between which visitors to the city would have entered. But now there is only one, which is merely a public rest room, serving as an entrance not to the city, but to this park for the people. If Ledoux could have foreseen the future of this building, perhaps he might have integrated the plumbing.

•　　■　　•

*Ile de la cité from Samaritaine rooftop café*

In addition to visiting Parc Monceau, I went to the rooftop café of the Samaritaine department store, where I looked out over Paris and reflected on my experiences in this magical city. The view was inspiring and offered a great panorama of Paris, as well as a close view of the heart of the city, whose monumental markers appear above the close-knit urban fabric. The

nearby Seine—the city's carrier of growth and rebirth—flows through and touches all areas of the city, representing a commonality among everything. The islands exude spirituality, with Notre Dame's rising towers, bold facade, and rose window; its central flamboyant spire pierces the sky, soaring toward the heavens as it has through much of France's complex history.

The powerful, slate-covered dome of the Panthéon, rising beyond the old chapel at the Sorbonne, is still a reminder of the intellectual center of Paris—the Latin Quarter. Though no one converses in Latin as they did many centuries ago, there is a balanced richness of languages from many different cultures permeating the Latin Quarter. This is particularly true at the Sorbonne, where students from around the world share ideas, and learn not of a monistic world, but of a complex, multifarious one.

The massive green roof of Garnier's Opéra on the Right Bank evocatively marks the world of materialism and commerce, whereas the Neoclassical Bourse, La Madeleine and its surrounding shops, and numerous banks still dominate the cityscape.

The Louvre on the Right Bank and the Musée d'Orsay on the Left Bank monumentally symbolize the arts and culture of Paris, and though they contain numerous works of art, they represent only a small percentage of the abundant richness that exists throughout the city.

The Montmartre area, marked by the domes of the Sacré Coeur, which is often shrouded in mist, still tries to cling to its artistic heritage, though it is more symbolic of gaiety and hedonism. Seediness still pervades the streets at the base of the hill, where delight is the ultimate aim.

The Pompidou Center, boldly visible in its brilliant polychromatic defiance of its traditional cream-colored stone neighbors, seems to breed a new form of art—or perhaps an art never before so visible. It shocks you, dares you to question it, to be involved with it, and though it is a haven for many lost souls, the whole world comes to it, and the vagrants who lay upon the ground of the surrounding square are but a small percentage of those who share in its madness.

And last, the Eiffel Tower rises above all, never losing its power, standing even more proudly than it did one hundred years ago when it was scorned by critics. It not only represents the wonder of science and technology, but has become a symbol for the whole of France, where beauty, progress, and preservation remain important values, where one notion does not overwhelm the other. Like France, the Eiffel Tower is clearly rooted, powerful, symmetrical, and balanced; yet it is not stagnant—it conveys movement and intricacy. What better symbol could a country desire?

# Bibliography

Barthes, Roland. *The Eiffel Tower and Other Mythologies*. Translated by Richard Howard. New York: Hill and Wang, 1979.

DeWitt, Dennis J., and Elizabeth R. DeWitt. *Modern Architecture in Europe—A Guide to Buildings Since the Industrial Revolution*. New York: E. P. Dutton, 1987.

Frampton, Kenneth. *Modern Architecture—A Critical History*. New York: Oxford University Press, 1980.

Honour, Hugh. *Neo-Classicism*. New York: Viking Penguin, 1977.

Hugo, Victor. *The Hunchback of Notre-Dame*. Translated by Walter J. Cobb. New York: New American Library, 1965.

Littlewood, Ian. *Paris: A Literary Companion*. New York: Harper and Row, 1988.

Michelin Tyre Public Limited Company. *Paris*. 5th ed. London: Michelin, 1985.

"New Architecture in Paris." *Progressive Architecture*, July 1987, 67–99.

Pevsner, Nikolaus. *Pioneers of Modern Design from William Morris to Walter Gropius*. New York: Viking Penguin, 1975.

Ruskin, John. *The Seven Lamps of Architecture*. New York: Dover Publications, 1989.

Salvadori, Renzo. *Architect's Guide to Paris*. Kent: Butterworth Architecture, 1990.

Van Zanten, David. *Designing Paris: The Architecture of Duban, Labrouste, Duc, and Vaudoyer*. Cambridge: Massachusetts Institute of Technology, 1987.

Wurman, Richard Saul. *Paris Access*. New York: Accesspress, 1990.

*Designed by James Stockton & Associates*
*Set in Weiss by Wilsted & Taylor*
*Printed and bound by South China Printing Co. Ltd.*